Praise For Clark Finnical's Writing

I've written more than 50 posts on LinkedIn...

Here's what people have said...

****

Best LinkedIn article in the last year. Thank you.

Sally Field, President and Owner, Sky's the Limit Coaching and Consulting

To be honest, I've never read such a comprehensive article on the art of job searching.

I can imagine you conducted tons of research to compile your finished piece.

This will not only become a reference for those seeking a job but for those who are employed and wish to assist their job seeking friends. Thank you for providing this information to the public for free.

Sonia Mercado, Supplier Diversity Manager SONY Metropolitan Transportation Authority

These suggestions are solid advice for jobseekers - and for all of us. Thank you.

Lynn Prinz, Assistant Director, Indiana University Southeast – Career Development Center

Best advice I've read in a long time.

Karen Parsons, Development Manager

Simple and Powerful - well spoken, Clark.

Jason Singer, Experis Executive Recruiter

Clark, you have a gift. Looking forward to reading.

LaJuana Porter, Sales/Business Development Relationship Manager

Thank you for hitting the nail on the head with a great article and some great thoughts as to how to get hired!

Patricia Jackley, Business Development Manager OIC of South Florida

Excellent. People really need to appreciate the value of this content. It is priceless.

Dilip Sahu, Global CEO, Founder, Principal--Women Empowerment

Wow this is an amazing article. Now I understand a lot of things. It is not easy... but thank you for sharing, I really appreciate it!

Mariluz Quiros, CPA, MSA, Assistant Accounting Manager

Thank you for sharing this must read! This is such a great way to go about updating a resume. Amazing post! Well written and remarkable!

Jennifer Siller-Lasry, Fitness-Fashionista

As always a marvellous thought provoking article.

Part of what I do is present to diverse work groups of varying levels about being mindful of negative self-talk.

You hit the nail right on the head with this. Thank you!

Liam Parfitt M.Res., M. Phil, CPE., BVC, Regional Manager, Supreme Court of Newfoundland and Labrador

You're on the mark with this article Clark.

Having been on both sides of this "fence", I can relate to the majority of the points you listed.

Managers spend an average of six seconds scanning resumes so you need to make those six seconds count. Good post!

Valerie D., Technical Publications Professional

Hi Clark, I read a few of your articles and I just want to say thank you so much for the excellent information.

I'm heading back in to the job search and am pretty shaky and uncertain, your articles are fantastic. Cheers, Jen

Jen Cochran, Marketing Strategist

Well said. Excellent advice from start to finish.

Bryan Holup MBA, MLHR, Sr. Human Resources Manager

Great insightful, thought out, and well written article that everyone needs to read whether they have a job or not.

Running Wolf, President at Savagely Twisted Records, LLC

Thank you so much for this amazing article.

Indeed looking for work is by far the hardest project I've ever been given from the universe.

It's people like you, willing to help and show kindness, that continue to give me hope.

AnnMarie Marcolin, RN BScN MHSc, Toronto, Ontario, Canada

I used Clark Finnical's excellent tips to improve my LinkedIn profile.

After applying the updates, the next week I received several emails and calls from recruiters, stating they had seen my LinkedIn profile and wanted to talk.

This was the first time any recruiter had ever mentioned my profile.

Thanks Clark, your tips led me to the technical job I have today!

Glenn Cate, Wireless Engineer

This is the most comprehensive article I have read on the what, why and how of writing a stand out [LinkedIn] headline. Well done.

Patricia Edwards, Top Ranked Career Coach at www.CareerWisdomCoach.com

Best article I've seen about maximizing your LI profile. Well done!!

Tricia Brock, Intel Global Strategic Sourcing Manager

What a great idea attaching your personality profile to your LI Profile.

I've even taken Strengths Finder myself.

I've recommended including language from the personality profile in your LI profile but I like your idea better of including excerpts.

Lisa Ann Landry, MSM, CEO of Paradigm Shifts Training & Development & Social Media Marketing Strategist.

As a CIO with an engineering and marketing background, I trust the data... And this is fascinating data. Thanks!

Wayne Sadin, Chief Information & Digital Officer, Affinitas Life

This is spot on. Most seem obvious to me, but I actually think about this stuff - a lot.

You also pointed out one excellent point that I hadn't thought of - the name@prestigious-alma-mater.

A great suggestion to highlight your education - and get the most mileage from those hefty student loans. :) Well done!

Julie Wienen Withrow, Marketing & Business Strategist at www.juliewithrow.com

I'm in that situation now, and think that your book will be "EXCELLENT" for all to read and understand the process.

Wishing you the Best of Luck and can't wait to read your book.

Thank you on behalf of all of us that are seeking employment!!

Sharon Bingert, Results Driven, Dynamic Tech Writer/Trainer in Telecommunications and Pharmaceutical Industries

Hello. Clark. I personally want to thank you for all of your posts on LinkedIn.

Your "shares" are inspiring and very helpful for hungry job applicants frequently on LinkedIn!

Kelsey Blakely, Relationship Management | Business Consulting

Hey, I never found Linked-in very important until today, thanks to Mr. Clark Fs' advice for job seekers.

Tegegnework Yirga, Private Consultant

Clark, Thank you so much for taking the time to post this very informative information!

It will help me immensely.

Phillip Isan, Pinpoint Planning, Consulting and Management

Brilliant!

Muna (Syeda Rahat) Haider, Art Facilitator

Job Hunting Secrets
(from someone who's been there)

Written By Job Search Veteran and Job Seeker Advocate

Clark Finnical

Copyright © 2017 The Job Seeker's Advocate LLC

All Rights Reserved.

5905 47th Avenue North, Suite C, St. Petersburg, FL 33709

IMPORTANT DISCLAIMER

Ordering Information

Quantity sales. Special discounts are available on quantity purchases by colleges, universities, associations and others. For details contact the publisher at the address above.

ISBN-13: 978-1978258211
ISBN-10: 1978258216

Job Hunting Secrets
(from someone who's been there)

Written By Job Search Veteran and Job Seeker Advocate

Clark Finnical

1. Job Hunting. 2. Careers. 3. Self-Help. 4. Motivation & Inspiration. 5. Business.

The stories about the people in the book do not use their actual names.

I've included a handful of affiliate links in the kindle version for highly recommended products.

Copyright Page

Dedication

To HB, without her patience, love and support, this book would never have been written.

Table of Contents

Why I Wrote 'Job Hunting Secrets (from someone's who's been there)'…………..16

Read This Warning Before Going On!…………………………………………………18

If You're Unsure About The Job You Want……………………………………..……19

The Lies, The Under-Informed, The Noise, Danger, and Lack of Understanding….21

The 12 Lies Told To Job Seekers……………………………………………………22

The Under-Informed……………………………………………………………....29

The Noise You Need To Ignore……………………………………………………......30

    Conflicting & Questionable Sources…………………………………………30

    The News………………………………………………………………………..30

The Danger You Need To Be Aware Of……………………………………..………32

Their Inability To Understand……………………………………………………33

How To Increase Your Chance Of Landing A Job 500%……………………………34

The Most Widely Known Path………………………………………………………35

    My Experience With the HR Elimination System……………………………36

    Employees Are Paid To Provide Referrals…………………………………36

    Networking Beats The HR Elimination System Every Time…….……………..……36

Staffing Companies…………………………………………………………….…...37

Recruiters…………………………………………………………………………37

Contacting the Hiring Manager……………………………………………………38

The Wisdom of Pursuing Other Paths……………………………………………..…38

The Hiring Manager's Secrets…………………………………………………40

Secret #1 - 3 Questions That Determine If You Are A Candidate………………….…..40

Secret #2 - 4 Ways To Differentiate Yourself From All Other Candidates…………41

Secret #3 - The Third Secret Follows From 1 & 2…………………………………41

How To Have A Successful Mindset…………………………………43

Your Reaction to Your Circumstances…………………………………..43

Your Self-Talk…………………………………46

Your Self-Image…………………………………48

Knowing Yourself………………………………….51

Your World View…………………………………51

Your Beliefs…………………………………..52

The Impact of Others' Opinions…………………………………53

Before Going Any Further…………………………………54

Before You Can Be Successful, You Need To Know What Failure Looks Like…….....55

Impress Hiring Managers With Your Achievement Stories………………………..………56

Responsibilities or Achievements?…………………………………58

What is an Achievement Story?…………………………………58

How To Collect Your Achievement Stories…………………………………59

Understanding What Makes You Different…………………………………64

How to Quantify Achievement Stories………………………………….......65

How To Write Achievement Stories…………………………………67

How Achievement Stories Help You…………………………………..68

Where Are Achievement Stories Used?…………………………………71

What If I Don't Want To Brag?…………………………………72

Networking…………………………………73

Networking Defined…………………………………74

Successfully Starting A Networking Conversation…………………………………74

The Rewards of Small Talk…………………………………75

The H.E.R. Method – Created by Danielle D. Dupree……………………………………..76

Don't Forget These People In Your Network……………………………………………77

Finding Networking Events Worth Going To……………………………………………79

The Value of Weak Ties……………………………………………………………………80

Will Spelling Keep You Out of Interviews?………..………………………………….…82

Your Resume………………………………………………………………………………83

Create A Winning Resume………………………………………………….....……84

Why Omitting Your Address May Be A Wise Move……………………………………86

What Message Is Your Email Sending?…………………………………………………88

Create A Summary That Quickly Shows What You Have To Offer……………………..91

Accomplishments Create A Strong Work Experience……………………………………92

Education……………………………………………………………………………96

Awards, Skills, Certifications & Training……………………………………………98

How to Make Your Resume Easy to Read……………………………………………101

Up To 90% of All Applications Are Rejected Before A Human Reads Them………103

How To Get Through the HR Elimination System (ATS)………………....……….....103

The Quick Way To Customize Your Resume and Get Selected by the ATS….……105

Before Your Resume Goes Anywhere………………………………………………109

To Your Success…………………………………………………………………111

A Question For You…………………………………………………………….....113

Additional Reading………………………………………………...…………………114

Career Coaches……………………………………………………………………116

Keeping The Faith…………………………………………...……………………118

Acknowledgements……………………………………………………………………120

The Reason I Wrote...

'Job Hunting Secrets

(from someone who's been there)'

The premise of this book is simple, today's job seeking world exists to benefit those who play in that world every day or at least more often than the average job-seeker, namely, the recruiters, HR managers and hiring managers.

As a result, there are a lot of myths, misconceptions and sometimes, downright lies that put the job seeker at a disadvantage.[1]

This book was written to level that playing field because you deserve a better job search experience than mine.

I never felt like anyone was looking out for job seekers. That's why I wrote this book and that's why I've created, "The Job Seeker's Advocate LLC."

Because of my experiences I understand what you're going through in a way others who haven't been job seekers will never understand:

I was in the job market 5 times.

1. In 1989, my final year at school, I sent 60 resumes out. Most employers didn't respond. Those who did sent rejection letters. I didn't know what would happen until an on-campus interview. Thankfully, the recruiter was impressed, and I was ultimately hired.

2. In 1995, my division was put up for sale. We were told that most of our jobs would eventually be eliminated. Some lost jobs immediately. Thankfully I didn't. After scanning the corporate jobs system, I found the perfect match in another division and won over the hiring manager.

3. In 2002, this division restructured. My boss and I, along with many others, lost their jobs. I went off payroll. I had no idea what the future held. One Friday afternoon my

---

[1] I'm not saying everyone you'll deal with is solely out for themselves, I am saying the job seeker's interests are not their top priority.

old employer called. They needed my social security number. Only then did I learn that an interview two weeks earlier had converted into a job.

4. In 2010, during the Great Recession, everyone in my division from the Senior Vice-President to my boss lost our jobs over a 12-months period. I was off payroll for almost 6 months. Thankfully, God gave me the smarts to get referrals that led to interviews and a great job in a great department.

5. In 2012, when the recession combined with a shrinking market for my employer's products, my job was eliminated again. I spoke to 100 people, but there was no future for me in that company. Fortunately, a retirement package eased the transition.

With my employer of 24 years out of the picture, I applied for jobs in sunny Florida. After not getting any bites, I relocated my family to Florida, assuming that my out-of-state residence was the reason Florida employers hadn't responded to my applications. It wasn't.

In fact, not until I started working six months later, as a short-term contractor, did I start getting bites. Thankfully, my contract was renewed twice. During that time, I interviewed with a well-run company, where I work now, four years later.

In short, I'm one of you. Even though I'm happily employed today, I understand what you are feeling, thinking and experiencing because of what I've been through.

Few Things Are As Complex As Landing A Job

At its core, the principles behind landing a job, that is, how you win over the hiring manager, are relatively simple. The complexity lies in how you make that happen.

One of the things that kept me hired when so many people were losing their jobs — and got me hired after I lost mine — was my desire to master complex things.

Except for maybe nuclear physics and interstellar space travel, there are few things as complex as landing a job.

In spite of its complexity, the job search process was a nut I was determined to crack. With my wife homeschooling our kids, I had little choice. I had to solve this puzzle. I was committed.

Read This Warning Before Going On!

If you know anything about human nature, you'll understand the quote below.

New opinions are always suspected and usually opposed because they are not already common.

~ John Locke

In other words, if people haven't heard something in the past, they'll question it. What these folks are not considering is that new things are always coming around the corner, especially these days.

I share this warning because when you tell others what you've learned from reading my book, don't be taken aback if you hear, "I've never heard that before."

If you hear these words, you can tell them:

I'm not surprised. You've never heard words like these because HR veterans and recruiters were the only people writing books for job seekers in the past.

'Job Hunting Secrets (from someone who's been there)' was written by someone like me — someone whose job was eliminated, someone who adapted to his new circumstances and did what he had to do to land work.

He's been through this more times than he'd like to remember. However, because of his desire to learn all he can about the job search experience, I now have a book on conducting a successful job search written by someone who's been in my shoes, someone who knows exactly what I'm going through, someone who knows exactly what I'm thinking, someone who knows exactly what I'm feeling, and most importantly, someone who has done everything possible to help job seekers understand how to land work.

Don't get me wrong. I'm not trying to minimize the value of books written by Human Resources veterans and recruiters. In fact, as you read my book, you'll see I frequently include valuable insights from HR veterans and recruiters.

If You're Unsure About The Job You Want ...

Take the classes, the friends, and the family that have inspired the most in you. Save them in your permanent memory and make a backup disk. When you remember what you love, you will remember who you are. If you remember who you are, you can do anything.

~ Cartoonist Cathy Guisewite

I can help you AFTER you've decided on the type of job you will pursue. If this is you, consider reading one or more of these books:

What Color Is Your Parachute? by Richard Bolles, has sold more than 10,000,000 copies since its first publication. It is rewritten every year, and has been translated into 20 languages and published in 26 countries.

The book is more than job seeking as you can see in these chapters:

- Self-Inventory Parts 1 & 2
- The Five Ways To Choose / Change Careers
- How To Start Your Own Business
- Finding Your Mission In Life
- A Guide to Choosing a Career Coach or Counselor

The Pathfinder by Nicholas Lore uses the techniques of the Rockport Institute, Lore's career-guidance network, to make *The Pathfinder* a substitute for a job counselor. Through goal setting, list making, and other techniques, the book leads readers through deciding exactly what they want to do for a living and finding a way to make it happen.

The book consists of three parts:

- Living A Life You Love
- How To Get There From Here
- Designing Your Future Career

Do What You Are by Barbara Barron and Kelly Tieger. Richard Bolles, author of *What Color is Your Parachute?* says: "This is one of the most popular career books in the world. It's easy to see why. Many have found great help from the concept of Personality Type, and Tieger and Barron are masters at explaining this approach to career choice. Highly recommended."

The authors broke the book into three sections:

- Part One – Unlocking the Secrets of Personality Type
- Part Two – The "Fourmula" for Career Satisfaction
- Part Three – Getting to Work

Part Three has a chapter on each Myers Briggs Personality Type where it discusses the type of work preferred by each type.

The Lies, The Under-Informed, The Noise, Danger, and Lack of Understanding

Wisdom is the most important thing; therefore get wisdom: and with all your getting get understanding.

Proverbs 4:7

The 12 Lies Told To Job Seekers

The Truth Will Set You Free, But First It Will Piss You Off

~ Gloria Steinem

As job seekers, when we start our job hunt, we have no restrictions on what we can or cannot do. However, practically everyone we meet tells us what we have to do. The sad thing is that, because most job seekers don't know any better, they fall for what they hear.

I know I did. That's why I wrote this chapter. I'm not saying that everyone who speaks to you during your job hunt is lying.

What I am saying is that you need to be careful. Much of what is passed off as common knowledge or wise advice doesn't actually help you.

Much of what job seekers are told helps the person who is telling you.

OK, you're probably asking, "So what do I do?"

Don't be quick to accept everything you hear. When faced with decisions where you are uncertain …

… seek out people who are outside of the process,

… people who won't benefit from your decisions.

People who will genuinely care, for example, might be:

a parent, a relative, a professor or teacher, a former boss, a religious advisor, or anyone else who doesn't have a vested interest in the decisions you make.

And that's the criterion you should use: seek out someone who does *not* have a vested interest in your decision. (For instance, a parent who wants you "to turn out just like me" does have a vested interest.)

If you have to make a decision without the benefit of one of these people, don't rush that decision. Consider the pros and cons and then decide.

Side note: You may even use exercises for "weighting" the pros and cons. Some job counselors even suggest giving a numerical value to factors, putting them in the pros or cons column, and then adding to get a result.

For instance, in the FOR column, you might assign *a good location* the numerical value of 3 (out of 10), while *a solid company* might be an 8, and *a great boss* might be a 10. In the AGAINST column, *a poor location* might still be a 5, while *a startup company*, while exciting, may only get a 6, and a so-so boss might be a 7. Then add the results and see what you get.

One more thing, I'm not trying to bring you down by pointing out the lies you might be told. I'm trying to help you understand the people you'll be working with, so that you won't be manipulated by people who couldn't care less about your future, and so that you'll make decisions that are best for you.

Job Postings Say, "Do Not Contact The Hiring Manager"

This seems logical at first. However, the Application Tracking System rejects anywhere from 75% to 90% of applicants, and the system is notorious for misreading resumes.

So, if you receive an automated rejection letter, you have nothing to lose and potentially a lot to gain by contacting the hiring manager.

For instance, Kelly Kinnebrew, Ph.D, an Organizational and Leadership expert notes that:

"If you are targeted and make a strong case for why a contact would want to speak with you, I have found outreaches directly to hiring managers, VPs of talent and the like give back a reply probably 8 out of 10 times."

In other words, don't ever think the automated rejection has sealed your fate.

Besides, there is a widely held belief that the right hand of an organization knows what the left hand is doing. Don't believe it for a second.

Once, I received an automated rejection the day of an interview. The hiring manager never mentioned it, and I was in the running for the position for months. I've read LinkedIn posts where others have experienced the same thing.

External Recruiters Say, "Your Salary Expectations Are Way Too High"

As Liz Ryan, wisely points out:

"If personnel agency people and recruiters tell every job-seeker to lower their expectations, they'll have an easier time finding those job-seekers work -- and collecting their finder's fees from employers.

It's much easier to put people into low-paying jobs than high-paying jobs! Agencies have more low-paying jobs to fill than higher-paying ones."

Liz recommends vetting recruiters, so you can find one who appreciates what you have to offer instead of making you think you're worth less than you really are.[2]

One of my readers shared how she got the old bait-and-switch when she went to a large staffing company. When she first met with the company, the salaries were great. When she came back, those jobs were no longer available, but jobs paying half as much were available. The same thing happened to me the last time I was in the job market.

Human Resources Says, "Only Apply to Jobs If You Have 80% of the Requirements"

HR says this because it reduces the number of applications they have to review. The 80% requirement sounds logical, until:

- You read a job description, which is one continuous sentence and 15 lines long.

- The hiring manager says he's so busy that he didn't have time to create a job description. In fact, the description online is only a template, so it doesn't describe the actual job.

- The hiring manager tells you that they haven't fleshed out the responsibilities for the new role.

- The job requirements appear as if they're looking for a Nobel Prize winner.

    I've encountered all four situations.

    I've applied for positions where I didn't have 80% of the requirements. Because of the exposure I received during the interview, I was asked to interview for another role. That is where I work now, four years later. I know others who've done the same thing.

Hiring Managers say, "You Are A Top Candidate"

They tell you this because they want you to stop looking and focus on this role, so that you're still available when they actually make a decision.

What's worse, they may not know whether the top candidate will accept their offer or not. Hence, they need someone if the top candidate declines their offer. In fact, they may not know whether the top three candidates will accept the offer. For that reason, they may tell anywhere from three to ten applicants that they are top candidates.

---

[2] Ryan, Liz. "The recruiter said you need to lower your expectations." Forbes. https://www.forbes.com/sites/lizryan/2017/03/05/the-recruiter-said-you-need-to-lower-your-expectations/#7e8c8e33fa0e (accessed October 8, 2017).

Recruiters say, "You Must Put Your Address On Your Resume"

This sounds like a harmless request, at first. After all, people have put their addresses on resumes for years. As The Avid Careerist, Donna Svei, wisely notes, recruiters want your home address because studies show that a person with a one-hour commute has to earn 40% more money to be as happy with life as someone who walks to the office.

In-house recruiters know that people with long commutes often eventually quit "because of the commute." If the job holder quits, the recruiter appears incompetent and must go through the hiring process all over again.

As a result, candidates with commutes longer than what's viewed as tolerable often go to the "no" pile. Donna recommends giving the address of your current or most recent employer's city, instead.[3]

Hiring Managers say, "We'll Decide By The End Of The Month"

They tell you this because they're hoping it will make their position top in your mind. As a result, you'll be less likely to look elsewhere. In other words, they want you to still be available when they get around to deciding.

Even though some hiring managers may want to decide by the end of the month, there are many factors beyond the hiring manager's control.

I've seen this at my current work. We interviewed a great and well-liked candidate. However, the hiring manager was exceedingly busy responding to her boss's requests.

As a result, the candidate wisely landed another role with another company.

I attended church with someone who, before he was hired, had to tell his current employer, "It's been seven months. If you don't make a decision now, I'm moving on."

External Recruiters Say, "Great Work Culture!"

I'm always amused when I see recruiters do this.

---

[3] Svei, Donna. "The Real Reason You Shouldn't Put Your Address on Your Resume." Avid Careerist. http://www.avidcareerist.com/2014/02/02/address-on-resume/ (accessed October 8, 2017).

How would external recruiters know it's a great work culture? They don't work there.

Further, the fact that they're touting the work culture tells you something about the salary. If recruiters can't tout salary or benefits, the only thing left is the work culture.

Hiring Managers And Recruiters Say "You're Overqualified"

This is like being told, "That outfit doesn't make you look fat."

It sounds complementary, but it's hiding something.

"You're overqualified" is a standard response when the recruiter either doesn't want to or can't tell you why you didn't get the job.

Usually, recruiters don't want to tell you why you didn't get the job, because they don't want you to be mad at them, in case they have another role that is an ideal fit.

A LinkedIn connection recently told me that she wanted to work for a certain organization. She interviewed but was told that she was overqualified. She asked me why the recruiter would say such a thing.

After reading her message, I explained, as delicately as possible, that her English skills prevented her from landing the position.

A hiring manager told a close friend of mine that he was overqualified. My friend is a tall man with a deep voice. He's articulate, experienced, and capable. For all of these reasons, I believe he intimidated the hiring manager.

Many Websites Say, "You Have To Use Our Web Site To Find Jobs"

Websites say this because:

1. The greater the traffic on their site, the more they can charge advertisers.

2. The longer you stay on their site, the greater the likelihood you will purchase their services.

3. The more traffic on their site, the more information they will collect. The more information they collect; the more they can sell.

However, we all know that Google indexed the web. Thanks to Google, you can find the jobs you are interested in without going to multiple job boards. It's as simple as entering terms like these into the Google Search bar.

Tampa "Financial Analyst" -sql

When I clicked 'Search,' all of the Financial Analyst jobs in the Tampa area that do not require SQL were returned.

Jobs from Indeed, Monster, ZipRecruiter, LinkedIn, Citi, CareerBuilder, Randstad, Snagajob, JobScore, MetLife, and ParkerLynch were returned in the first two pages.

Try it. You'll be amazed at how easy it is.

Recruiters Say, "You Must Provide Your Salary History"

As Liz Ryan has pointed out in many articles, you don't have to provide your salary. If the recruiter insists, walk away.

Recruiters ask for this information, because they want to pay you as low a salary as possible. If you're currently working and you've told them you earn $50,000 a year, recruiters think you will accept an offer between $53,000 and $55,000.

If you're not working, they may believe that $50,000 is sufficient. The best indication of what you should be paid is the local market.

If you're a Wireless Engineer in Florida, for example, you can research the local market. Here are two responses:

Indeed — the average Wireless Engineer makes $96,636 in Florida.[4]

Glassdoor — the base salary for a Verizon Wireless Engineer in Tampa is $83,237.[5]

Based on this information, you could tell the recruiter, "I'm interested in Wireless Engineer positions in the Tampa Bay area with salaries ranging between $80,000 and $100,000."

As Liz Ryan notes, ethical recruiters will share the salary range with candidates and work with them.[6]

Many People Say, "One Strategy Will Always Land A Job"

---

[4] "Wireless Engineer Salaries in Florida." Indeed. https://www.indeed.com/salaries/Wireless-Engineer-Salaries,-Florida?from=mobsalaryblock (retrieved October 8, 2017).
[5] "Verizon Wireless Engineer Systems Salaries in Tampa, FL." Glassdoor. https://www.glassdoor.com/Salary/Verizon-Wireless-Engineer-Systems-Tampa-Salaries-EJI_IE11806.0,16_KO17,33_IL.34,39_IM850.htm (accessed October 8,2017).
[6] Ryan, Liz. "Five Lies Recruiters Tell Job-Seekers." Forbes. https://www.forbes.com/sites/lizryan/2016/01/06/five-lies-recruiters-tell-job-seekers/2/#6f9e8b7f7180 (accessed October 8, 2017).

Let's think about our logic here. If there is truly one strategy that always lands a job, don't you think we'd already know about it?

Don't you think when people discovered how it worked, word would get around and spread like wildfire?

Don't you think that as more and more people used the same strategy, it would lose its effectiveness?

One more question: Given how different everyone is, that people have different values, beliefs, and experiences, and that companies are full of all kinds of people, why would one strategy work with all of them?

Does the door to door salesman get invited into every home?

Do presidential candidates ever get everyone's vote?

People who tell you this one strategy is guaranteed to work 100% of the time are selling a dream with little connection to reality.

If someone starts telling you one strategy works all of the time, start walking away. They obviously have no respect for you and are only interested in what you will part with to hear this so-called strategy.

Some People Say, "You Can't Afford To Screw Up"

The bottom line is that everybody screws up. Sometimes I think God has me screw up to protect me from bad situations that I can't see.

I came into a staffing company once and met with one of their recruiters. When I called the staffing organization a week later, the recruiter I'd met with had moved on. I was referred to someone for whom English was a second language.

When she had to start spelling out words because I couldn't understand her and I couldn't understand the letters she was saying because she pronounced them differently, I started to lose it. Of course, it didn't help that the high paying positions that I was told about were no longer available.

Well, given that I offended one person at one staffing firm in a metropolitan area of 2.8 million people, I'm not going to lose sleep over it. Perhaps they will learn not to tell candidates they have $100,000 salary positions, when the closest thing they have pays only half of that. Anyway, while I never wish any ill toward anyone, it was probably good for me to blow off some steam.

The Under-Informed...

I saw this continuously when I was a job seeker. I'd call a friend working for a great company and make the mistake of asking him, "Do you know of any good job opportunities at your company?"

He responded, "Oh no, they've been eliminating jobs for years."

After hanging up, I went to his employer's career site and found page upon page of good jobs, many of which I could apply for.

When you worked for your last employer, did you know anything about open positions outside of your department?

Unless you worked in HR or were actively looking for a new position there, you knew nothing.

It's easy to think, "They work there, and they're closer to it than I am, so they should know." In reality, they rarely know more than you. If they do know more, it's rarely a full picture of all of the opportunities.

TAKEAWAY

1. Don't ask people who don't know.

2. Don't listen to people who don't know.

Believe me, everyone and their brother, cousin, great aunt (you get the idea) will be only too happy to give you their opinions.

So, after you've read the resume section and created your resume, and one of these people tells you, "You've done it all wrong," ask that person, "When was the last time you hired someone? When was the last time you interviewed someone?"

If you don't feel inclined to pose these questions, make a beeline for the door or turn up the volume on your ear buds.

A few years ago when I was in between roles, I messaged a former co-worker and made the mistake of asking her about jobs in the Tampa Bay area.

She replied, "There are no jobs in Tampa Bay."

She was obviously misinformed or at least under-informed, because I had a phone interview for a position in Tampa Bay the next day.

In short, don't be quick to assume that the people you're communicating with are the best source of information. Do you really want to make what could be life-impacting decisions based on people whose knowledge is limited?

It is in your moments of decision that your destiny is shaped.

~ Tony Robbins

The Noise You Need To Ignore

Avoid the confusing and unnecessary. If you can't avoid it, take advice from these stories:

Conflicting & Questionable Sources

One of the more challenging aspects of my own job searches and my research into job hunting is the conflicting information I've read.

For example, expert Jack Smith says that you must write a cover letter this way. Recruiter Dotty Jones says if you write the cover letter that way, she'll put it in the circular file.

I used to be confused when I read these conflicting stories, until I realized that Jack was telling me what he likes, and Dotty is telling me what she doesn't like.

In other words, their advice is of tremendous value only if Jack and Dottie are the people you work with during your career search.

With all of the websites and the pressure to put something out there, extensive reading will show you that the quality of what you read varies widely.

I'll never forget seeing a post in LinkedIn titled, "Is An MBA Really Worth It?" My greatest concern in seeing this post was that someone would follow the not so subtle message in that title.

Having worked in a company where in one department everyone who didn't have an MBA lost their job, I hate seeing posts like this. This was just one more example of an opinion that got into print that should be viewed with a great deal of skepticism.

In other words, you can't make life decisions based on one post in LinkedIn. We all need to get wisdom and get understanding before we make important decisions.

That is the purpose of this book, to give you the benefit of my experience and my research. In other words, I've sought to give you what I wished I had when I was between jobs.

The News

It seems logical to assume we should watch the news. After all, shouldn't we be in the loop about what's going on? If this were 1960, I'd agree with you.

A lot has changed in my lifetime. Because the media is a business, its top objective is maximizing advertising revenues. I've seen the impact of this first hand.

A few years back when I lived an hour north of Philadelphia, we knew who owned the local television station. His grandchildren went to the same school as our kids.

So I wasn't surprised one day when the weatherman said, in so many words, don't believe what the Philly stations are saying, there won't be a big snow storm. I knew what he was talking about, because I was watching Oprah on one of Philadelphia's network-owned stations. The show was frequently interrupted with messages telling their listeners, "Big storm coming. Tune in at 6:00 to find out about the big storm."

Author and entrepreneur, James Altucher, in his book, *I Was Blind But Now I See*, suggests that, *the best thing you can do is avoid all news.*

He explains why he's qualified to give that advice:

I've worked for over a dozen media companies. I've written for newspapers, TV shows, I've been a pundit on TV shows ... so I know what they are up to.

He goes on to share that he was backstage at a news show when the producer told him:

Don't fool yourself – all of this is just filler in between advertisements.

He elaborates:

Every week, a newsroom gets all of their best reporters and editors together on a Monday morning. Then the top guy says, "Ok, what have you got?" And the reporters have to respond with items that are designed to induce more and more terror. When the top guy thinks the terror is sufficient to beat out the competition, he says, "Ok, let's go with it."[7]

Some media outlets are guiltier of this than others.

Some of you may remember a picture floating around Facebook a couple years ago; basically, it said something like this:

1999 - FEAR Y2K

2000 – FEAR CHINA

2001 – FEAR OSAMA BIN LADEN

2002 – FEAR SADDAM HUSSEIN

2003 FEAR WEAPONS OF MASS DESTRUCTION

These words illustrate exactly what Altucher was talking about.

---

[7] Altucher, James. *I Was Blind But Now I See.* New York: CreateSpace. 2011. p. 35.

A few years back I watched a conversation in McDonalds between a young cashier and an older gentleman at least twice his age. The young cashier said,

It's really bad. I'm concerned.

The older gentleman responded,

This will pass. We'll get through it.

The young cashier believed the media. Because the older gentleman's years had enabled him to compare the reality he experienced with the media's headlines, he had a better understanding of what was really going on.

I share these stories because I don't want the media's headlines to scare you. The purpose of this chapter is to help you understand the world you are living in so you can make wiser decisions.

The Danger You Need To Be Aware Of

How I Was Ripped Off

When I was in between jobs many years back, I pursued a role and didn't get it. After landing a position, I attended a training class led by someone who worked in the same building as those I would have worked with had I gotten that job.

He told me that department was brutal. Perhaps, I should have picked up on that when I asked one question and then the hiring manager abruptly ended the interview. In retrospect, I believe God was protecting me.

I have to admit, at the time, I was little down after this happened. One day while reading LinkedIn I saw an ad offering 'free' training. I attended. The huckster told me his program would get me hired. I fell for it, hook line and sinker.

After spending around $400 twice, I learned what its like to work with someone who has no morals. He made a lot of promises and kept about 10% of them. He attempted to portray himself as a career expert and was anything but.

He gave us emails for 1500 new LinkedIn connections. He never took the time to explain why the connections were valuable. I couldn't help wondering whether these 1500 people paid him to give us their emails.

The clincher came when we were told we could listen to presentations from 10 experts. Interestingly enough, we were told to hold our questions until the end. When the end came, there was hardly any time for questions.

Desiring to follow up with one of the speakers, I contacted him directly. I told him I wanted to follow up after today's presentation. The speaker said he hadn't made a presentation today. It was then that I realized, we had been watching a recording of an earlier presentation, and we would never be able to ask questions.

How To Avoid Being Ripped Off

Look for the tactics the scam artist used to rip me off.

- They tell you next to nothing during the "free" training. In other words, if you want any help at all, start handing over the dough.

- They go on and on about how hard it is to land a job these days. In other words, you'd better sign up now, or you'll never get a job.

- They use the 'scarcity' strategy to corral you into signing up. They do this by telling you that there are a limited number of seats and that you have to sign up in the next 30 seconds, or you'll lose your chance.

Researching a business before you spend is wise. Keep in mind that people pay businesses to stuff the Internet with positive stories, so the bad stuff is sometimes pushed to page 50.

Here's how you can find the bad stuff on page 50 and beyond.

Go to the Google Search bar and enter these terms:

Scam OR ripoff OR complaint OR review OR "Better Business Bureau" OR BBB OR fraud "Potential Scammer's Name."

These sites can also provide helpful info:

https://www.sitejabber.com/reviews/

http://www.ripoffreport.com/

https://www.consumer.ftc.gov/articles/0243-job-scams - Signs

https://www.collegerecruiter.com/blog/2017/03/16/the-job-seekers-guide-to-identifying-and-avoiding-job-search-scams/ - more-233209.

Their Inability To Understand

One of the more challenging parts of being unemployed is how others can't understand what you are going through. In fact, no one understands unless they've been through it.

I'm not sharing this to get you down. It's simply a fact that we as job seekers need to accept, understand and then move on.

How To Increase Your Chance Of Landing A Job 500%

The Most Widely Known Path

If you're like most people, you believe landing an interview is limited to these three steps:

1.) Applying online,

2.) HR reviewing your application, and

3.) If your application is selected, the hiring manager reviewing it.

You believe this because almost everything you've read comes from current or former HR folks.

This process has significant flaws.

Because the Internet made applying for positions easy, HR was drowning in applications. As a result, the HR Elimination system was born.

That's not its official name, but the name fits. The official name is Applicant Tracking System or ATS. ATS systems reject, on average, 75% of all applicants. Sometimes the rejection rate can be as high as 90%.

J. P. Medved, content director at Capterra, a firm that helps companies find the right software for their business, said,

Reducing the number of candidates might seem good if we're weeding out irrelevant resumes...In reality, many of these rejected candidates were knocked out of the running for bad reasons. An automated system, like an ATS, will sometimes reject people for very minor reasons, like incorrect resume formatting. [8]

Bersin & Associates, an Oakland-based firm specializing in talent management, tested an ATS system. They created the perfect resume for an ideal candidate for a clinical scientist position. Matching the resume to the job description from a leading manufacturer, they submitted the resume to an applicant tracking system.

The ATS lost one of the candidate's work experiences. It also failed to read several educational degrees. As a result, the perfect resume for a clinical scientist position earned a score of 43, because the applicant tracking system misread it. [9]

---

[8] Kosinski, Matthew. "Do You Love Your ATS? Your Candidates Probably Hate It." Recruiter.com. https://www.recruiter.com/i/do-you-love-your-ats-your-candidates-probably-hate-it/ (Accessed October 8, 2017).

[9] Mason, Seth. "Another Biz Reporter Rips Applicant Tracking Systems". Ecominoes. http://www.ecominoes.com/2014/04/another-biz-reporter-rips-applicant.html (Accessed October 8, 2017).

Similarly, a Vice-President of Human Resources decided to test his company's ATS system. He applied for a job at his own company and received an automated rejection letter from the ATS.

My Experience With the HR Eliminations System

I applied to a firm, received the automated rejection letter the morning of the interview, and met with the hiring manager that afternoon. I was in the running for that position for two months. The reason I got an interview, in spite of the ATS, was that a friend of mine who worked at the firm advocated on my behalf.

A Very Effective Path

Adam Hyder, Head of Technology at Jobvite, a leader in Talent Acquisition software, analyzed Jobvite's customer data set. Adam found that while referrals make up only 6% of the applicant pool, they accounted for 39.9% of hires.[10]

Employees Are Paid To Provide Referrals

As Rob Paone, a former recruiter with experience in the technology staffing industry, points out, companies previously paid staffing firms $10,000 to $30,000 per candidate. Now they offer incentives of anywhere from $100 to $5000 to their employees to refer candidates.[11]

Referrals & Networking

Referrals and Networking have the same objective. Referrals enable someone to earn a referral fee if they recommend you. Networking seeks to get a recommendation but without the incentive fee.

Networking Beats The HR Elimination System Every Time

---

[10] Van Nuys, Amanda. "New Data: What You Didn't Know about Employee Referrals". Jobvite. http://www.jobvite.com/blog/new-data-what-you-didnt-know-about-employee-referrals/ (accessed October 8, 2017).

[11] Balogun, James. "Job Seekers: Use Employee Referral Programs to your advantage". Careerdreaming. http://careerdreaming.com/employee-referral-program/ (accessed October 8, 2017).

In a LinkedIn post, Lynda Spiegel shared that she submitted her resume to two different companies, both looking for a senior level human resources executive with global experience.

Lynda's experience matched most of the requirements. However, within hours of hitting "send," she received emails from both companies telling her there were other candidates more qualified for the position.[12]

Fortunately, Lynda had used her connections to send her resume to the hiring managers at both firms. Within one day of the ATS rejection, she received calls from these hiring managers asking her to interview based on the strength of her resume.

Staffing Companies

Staffing firms are hired by companies to vet candidates. Many of the top employers in my area use staffing firms to vet candidates for open positions.

The last time I was in the job market, I got a call from a local staffing firm fifteen days before I started my new job.

When I met with the firm, though, I found there was one big problem. Since I had already applied to the leading companies in my area, the staffing firm could not earn a commission by recommending me to their clients.

In fact, twelve months had to pass since my last application for the Staffing firm to earn a commission by recommending me.

I'm sharing this strategy early in the book, because pursuing this option could cut months off your job search.

Recruiters

The last time I was out of work, I invested a lot of time in my LinkedIn profile. As a result, even after I landed the job where I currently work, recruiters continued to call me.

Recruiters can be very helpful, even if they're only offering a temporary position. Here's why.

Recruiters can transform unemployed candidates into hot commodities. For instance, the last time I was in the job market, recruiters were contacting me, but they weren't offering permanent positions.

---

[12] Spiegel, Lynda. "Outfoxing the ATS: Can Software Finesse Software?" LinkedIn. Jul 10, 2015 https://www.linkedin.com/pulse/outfoxing-ats-can-software-finesse-lynda-spiegel (accessed October 8, 2017).

I was unemployed, and my applications were going nowhere. I had previously spoken with a staffing firm about a permanent position. Now that months had passed, I reached out to the recruiter and told him I was interested in a contractor role.

Within two weeks I was working. Because I was working, companies wanted to talk to me. I started getting interviews. Five months after starting the contractor role, I landed a permanent position. I've held it for four years now.

Contacting the Hiring Manager

I have also contacted hiring managers directly. Sometimes it's as simple as calling the company and saying I want to speak to Joseph Hiring Manager. The voice recognition or 'type the name' systems that are so common today are best, because they won't ask why you're calling.

Once, when I called a hiring manager directly, I got three interviews. Because I took the effort to call, I became a known quantity. I differentiated myself from the other candidates who didn't call.

The Wisdom of Pursuing Other Paths

When you only apply online, you're betting your future on the Applicant Tracking System. I know I'm repeating myself, however it's critical that you understand this. ATS systems reject, on average, 75% of all applicants. The percentage can be as high as 90%.

When you pursue career opportunities through networking, staffing companies, recruiters, or calling the hiring manager, your future is no longer in the hands of the HR Elimination System.

In other words, you significantly increase your chances of landing a job.

Orville Pierson, a former Vice President at Lee Hecht Harrison, the largest outplacement firm in the U.S. and author of three job search books, provides these success rates:

Networking or "Just Plain Talking To Other People" as Pierson likes to call it, is responsible for 75% of all hires. Pierson says networking enables you to become a known candidate, either as a referral or recommendation from an internal employee. Nothing makes a candidate more valuable than being known.

Staffing Firms and Executive Recruiters are responsible for 10% of positions that job hunters find. Employment agencies, "temp" firms, executive recruiters, and other staffing firms fill job openings for a commission, which is usually between 15% to 33% of the annual salary. The employer pays the fee.

The remaining 15% of jobs come through online applications and recruiters who are not Executive recruiters.[13]

As job seekers, if we complete three online applications a day, it's easy to fool ourselves into thinking we're being productive. So here's my question:

Given that "Talking To Other People" yields five times the number of jobs as online applications (75% vs. 15%), and staffing companies yield almost as many opportunities as online applications (10% vs. 15%),

Don't we owe it to ourselves to pursue these avenues?

If not for ourselves, then maybe for our loved ones who depend on us and our salaries.

---

[13] Pierson, Orville. *The Unwritten Rules of the Highly Effective Job Search*. New York: McGraw-Hill Education. 2006. Multiples pages.

The Hiring Manager's Secrets

Life is really simple, but we insist on making it complicated.

~ Confucius

Like all job seekers I always wanted to know:

What does it take to land a job?

I've had more opportunities than most to ask that question and search for that answer.

With my former employer's industry contracting and the economic downturns we've all been through, I've learned a lot.

In spite of the turmoil, in many ways those years were good, very good, in fact.

At my former employer, when one division was shrinking and my job was eliminated, I found work in a growing division. In spite of the musical chairs, I was promoted three times, and my salary tripled.

I'm not trying to brag. I'm trying to communicate that there is a way through the hell of losing your job.

After extensive reading, I feel like the MOST IMPORTANT ADVICE is always left out…the most important being…

… Understand How the Hiring Manager Thinks

Secret #1

3 Questions That Determine If You Are A Candidate

Can You Do The Job?

Will You Like The Job Enough To Stay There?

Can We Stand To Work With You?

Secret #2

4 Ways To Differentiate Yourself From All Other Candidates:

Have You Made Money For Your Employers?

Have You Saved Money For Your Employers?

Have You Increased the Productivity of Your Employers?

Have You Make A Difference at Your Employers?

Everything I did before, during and after the interview was geared toward answering those questions in as much detail as possible.

Secret #3

The Third Secret Follows From 1 & 2

Everything you do should be done so that the hiring manager feels totally comfortable asking you to join her team.

For that reason, here are things you should never say:

"Sorry I'm late."

Your lateness communicates that this job is not that important to you. It also communicates that you're not organized, and therefore, you're not dependable.

"Do you mind if I get this?"

If you decide to take a call during an interview, you've communicated that this job is not that important to you. (The only reason a hiring manager might excuse this behavior is if your parent or spouse is deathly ill.)

"I'm applying for this job because it will give me ..."

Don't talk about what the job can do for you. Talk about what you can do for the company.

"I'm not sure if I'm a good fit for this job, but ..."[14]

There are few things more foolish than expressing doubt about a job in an interview. The interview is the time to sell yourself and all you have to offer.

If you express doubt, you will make the hiring manager write you off. After all, she's trying to fill a role, so why should she waste time on someone with doubts?

"I need …"

The interview is not a time to talk about your needs. It is your time to explain how you can address the hiring manager's needs.

"How much paid time off do I get during the first year?"

Asking about time off gives the hiring manager the impression that you'll take as much time off as you can. Even if this is true, sending this type of message doesn't help you.

"I'm getting divorced/pregnant/going through a tough time."[15]

You'll never sell yourself to a hiring manager if you say things that make her think you'll be distracted and not able to focus on the job.

If you're uncertain about whether you should say something to the hiring manager or not, put yourself in her shoes and consider how such comments will make her feel.

_____

[14] The first four things you should never say came from Conlan, Catherine. "7 Things You Should Never Say During a Job Interview." Monster. https://www.monster.com/career-advice/article/never-say-during-job-interview (accessed October 8, 2017).

[15] The last three questions you should never say came from Smith, Jacqueline. "13 Things You Should Never Say In A Job Interview." Business Insider. http://www.businessinsider.com/never-say-these-things-in-a-job-interview-2014-8 (accessed October 8, 2017).

How To Have A Successful Mindset

You Might Be Tempted To Skip This Chapter...

... that is, until you never get called for an interview, OR your interviews don't go well.

Just as job seekers become more valuable by learning new skills, job seekers become more successful by adopting new ways of thinking. Here's why I say this.

Few things affect us more than how we think, yet how many of us take time to consider, "Is my thinking helping or hurting my situation?"

We frequently believe that success comes from following a few, well thought out, steps. When we think this way, we're ignoring how our thoughts drive everything we do.

The famed defender of France, Joan of Arc, said:

All battles are first won or lost, in the mind.

Are Your Thoughts On Your Side?

Let's answer this question by considering seven things...

Your Reaction to Your Circumstances

Are You Bitter About Your Job Loss?

That which you cannot release, possesses you.
~Andre Gide

Jeremy, a co-worker, lost his job just as I did in 2010. I called him one day and was amazed at his bitterness. In a few minutes, I learned how everything and everyone was unfair.

Since Jeremy had the option to relocate with his department but chose not to, I was surprised by his reaction.

When he eagerly spoke of networking events — where I would, once again, hear how unfair everything is — I quickly decided I was busy.

Except for two positions lasting 5 months each, Jeremy was out of work for 4 years.

Peggy McKee of Career Confidential, puts it this way:

You can be completely in the right; you can be treated unfairly; the deck can be stacked against you ... but your answer is not to be angry or bitter.

Bitterness will keep you from going after opportunities, and it will make you say things in job interviews that hurt you (trashing your old boss, not speaking in a positive way about failures or setbacks, etc.).

What is the answer? Keep moving. Move on to the next opportunity. Widen your net. Contact more hiring managers. Find the place and the position where you and your skills will be valued.[16]

Are You Depressed About Your Job Loss?

All the days of the desponding and afflicted are made evil [by anxious thoughts and forebodings], but he who has a glad heart has a continual feast [regardless of circumstances].

Proverbs 15:15 AMP

Rhonda, a co-worker of mine, was never the same after her layoff.

After my job was eliminated and I was hired back by our employer, Rhonda asked if ABCCO had any jobs. Then she said, 'They don't want any of the people they laid off.'

I replied, "That wasn't my experience nor the experience of Dusty, a mutual friend who was also hired back."

I never heard from her again. If her LinkedIn profile is any indication, she's not working or if she is, she doesn't want to share what she's doing.

Feeling Bad About Your Job Loss? Don't - Here's Why

If your experience is anything like mine, you've worked for excellently run companies as well as companies we wouldn't consider excellent.

Before you feel bad about your job loss, consider what the father of the quality movement, W. Edwards Deming, said:

A bad system will beat a good person every time.

Jim Collins, author of "Good to Great" and "Built to Last," shared these words about companies that succeed and those that do not. I'm paraphrasing:

---

[16] McKee, Peggy. "Monday Motivator for Your Job Search - Never Succumb to the Temptation of Bitterness." Career Confidential. http://careerconfidential.com/monday-motivator-for-your-job-search-never-succumb-to-the-temptation-of-bitterness/ (accessed October 8, 2017).

Leaders of great companies are modest and understated, while leaders with gargantuan egos led to either the demise of their companies or their continued mediocrity.[17]

When you think about your job loss, remember what Deming and Collins said.

In other words, don't sell yourself short because of the mistakes or short-sightedness of others.

Now that you have the opportunity, seek out truly great companies.

Are You Grateful?

If you're out of work, you might say, "What should I be grateful for?"

Well, when I was out of work, I was grateful for:

(1)   My loving wife
(2)   My son
(3)   My daughter
(4)   My faith
(5)   My health.

Studies prove choosing to be grateful will:

(1)   Make us happier.
(2)   Make people like us.
(3)   Make us healthier.
(4)   Boost our career.
(5)   Strengthen our emotions.

Want to discover more of the benefits of gratefulness? Check out this great article: "The 31 Benefits of Gratitude You Didn't Know About: How Gratitude Can Change Your Life."

http://happierhuman.com/benefits-of-gratitude/

Reframing

---

[17] Collins, Jim. *Good to Great: Why Some Companies Make the Leap...And Others Don't.* New York: HarperBusiness. 2001. p. 39.

Reframing is a way of viewing and experiencing events, ideas, concepts and emotions to find more positive alternatives.[18]

For example, if Jeremy were to reframe what happened to him, he would realize he has no reason to be bitter. In fact, since he was told his department was relocating, he shouldn't have even been surprised.

If Rhonda were to reframe what happened to her, she would no longer be depressed about her job loss. She would realize that job elimination is a normal part of any industry that is contracting, particularly during a recession.

When you examine the achievements in my Linkedin profile in light of my four job eliminations; the only logical explanation is a reduced demand for my employer's products and economic downturns.

In other words what happened to us is not because of us, factors beyond our control caused these job losses.

Your Self-Talk

Your self-talk — what you say to yourself throughout the day — can have a tremendously positive or negative impact. David Newman has some excellent advice for all of us:

Your mind will always believe everything you tell it.

Feed it hope.

Feed it truth.

Feed it with love.

Do you listen to what you say to yourself? Is your self-talk helping or hurting you?

It is essential that your self-talk builds you up and never tears you down.

If this is an issue, ask a friend to hold you accountable and check in with you once a week.

---

[18] "Cognitive reframing". Wikipedia. https://en.wikipedia.org/wiki/Cognitive_reframing (accessed October 8, 2017).

My Recent Self-Talk

A VP recently asked me to implement a significant change in a weekly report. While what he asked for wasn't easy, I was eager to make the improvements.

As I made these changes, I told myself:

This is great. I'm going to be more efficient, I'm going to get more done, I'm going to learn more and I'm going to be more valuable to my department.

Because of this self-talk, I was excited about the changes and more effective in implementing them.

My Job Seeking Self-Talk

While job seeking, I reviewed my accomplishments in detail. This reminded me of the great things God has enabled me to do. It also reminded me of the value I can bring to any employer. I also told myself:

It could be a lot worse. I could be fighting in Iraq or Afghanistan. I could be deathly ill. I could have a horrible wife and horrible kids.

By thinking these thoughts, I was able to put this chapter of my life in perspective and do what I needed to do to move on to the next chapter.

Cynthia Shapiro's take on Self-Talk

Cynthia Shapiro, in her wonderful book, *What Does Somebody Have to Do to Get A Job Around Here?* says:

What you're telling yourself with your inner voice comes through in every stage of your job search process.

When you have negative or insecure self-talk constantly running through your head, it will tend to govern the tone of your cover letters, e-mails, phone screenings, and interviews.[19]

Cynthia shares how successful athletes visualize getting baskets, making touchdowns, or hitting home runs.

Job seekers need to do the same thing. We need to visualize succeeding in interviews, excitedly sharing our achievement stories, and enjoying getting to know hiring managers and their teams.

Your self-talk plays an incredible role in your life. If you say anything that sounds the least bit negative, STOP yourself, and say:

---

[19] Shapiro, Cynthia. *What Does Somebody Have to Do to Get A Job Around Here?* New York: St. Martin's Press, 2008. Kindle location 3410.

I'm better than that. I'm capable and talented.

I'm going to share my achievement stories with hiring managers and help them understand how I can help them solve their problems.

Your Self-Image

One of the Most Important and Best Kept Secrets

I looked up "valuable" recently. It means "having desirable or esteemed characteristics or qualities."

While I now believe I'm a valuable person and employee, that wasn't always the case.

I know I'm not alone. Please remember: if you don't think you're valuable, it can undermine your job search.

You can't win over the hiring manager if you don't see your own value.

If you don't see your own value, you're more likely to give up.

Why People Don't Think They Are Valuable - People In Their Lives

As I think about what makes people not believe in themselves, I believe the single biggest reason is what they hear from the people in their lives.

Take my friend, Carl. Carl is an introvert born into a family of extroverts. Carl's father was very critical of Carl and never at a loss for words. Carl's brothers and sisters were just like their Dad.

Carl had a hard time growing up. No matter what he did, he was wrong in the eyes of his family. He wasn't only wrong. He was laughed at and ridiculed.

The people Carl grew up with believe that, "My way is the only way," and "I understand the ways of the world."

What they haven't considered, or may be unwilling to consider, is that their knowledge and experience is limited. They don't understand the world is made up of many unique and beautiful people.

One of the worst things Carl and those in similar situations can do is believe what these people say. This can be hard to avoid when the message is beaten into them day after day.

When we take in their messages, we let others decide how valuable we are. If this happens, we end up doing much less in our life than if we believed in ourselves.

Believing the negative things others say about us is a mistake. It is a mistake, because no one understands you and your value better than you do.

I once had a boss who said that I shouldn't be in the business world. She even sent me to a counselor to see if he agreed. He didn't.

At one point she said that I could be fired at any time because I made mistakes. When I discovered her own mistakes, she never said another word.

During the time I worked for that employer, my salary tripled, I was promoted three times, I received many awards, and I added $10M to the company's bottom line.

She obviously did not know what she was talking about.

I share this story because the people who are saying negative things about you don't know what they're talking about either.

If there are people in your life who don't appreciate you, get away from them as quickly as possible.

I also share these stories because I want you to believe in yourself. You're too valuable to live less of a life because others don't see your value.

Keep in mind; that your value doesn't decrease based on someone's inability to see your worth. Remember what Mark Twain said,

Keep away from people who try to belittle your ambitions. Small people always do that, but the really great make you feel that you, too, can become great.

Why People Don't Think They Are Valuable - Losing Your Job

I believe losing your job is the second biggest reason job seekers question their value.

I can tell you from personal experience that I have seen the most capable people lose their job.

At a former employer, a key subject matter expert was laid off. When the company realized what they had done, they tried to get her back. But she wasn't budging.

If you research the people who've lost their job you would find these famous people:

Walt Disney

J.K. Rowling

Michael Bloomberg

Oprah Winfrey

Thomas Edison.

So, the bottom line is: you're in good company. Some of the most talented people in the world have lost their jobs. Now it's your chance to be famous. Remember:

You Are Capable of Great Things - Believe It - Know It - Live It

Are You a Legend In Your Own Mind?

How many of you are or have been a "Legend in your own mind?"

True Confessions: Not too long ago, I was a legend in my own mind — impressed by my own work, even telling my boss how I am different from others and gifted. Really? *Yes, really.*

When I finally finished a major project and looked at the work others in our department were doing, reality began to overtake my earlier delusion. If I am gifted, why does the Director always go to Scott for special projects? If I am so capable, why is Mary my boss, and not vice versa?

As I rediscovered reality, I found a quote that embodied my new attitude:

The only way to be an expert is to never stop being a student.

As job seekers, we need to embody humility in all we do. Few things turn off a hiring manager more than a candidate who is full of himself.

What Is Your Locus of Control?

This fancy phrase means:

*The extent to which people believe they have power over events in their lives. A person with an internal **locus of control** believes he or she can influence events and their outcomes, while someone with an external **locus of control** blames outside forces for everything.*[20]

A person with an internal locus of control will be significantly more successful in his or her job search than someone with an external locus of control.

I have an internal locus of control. I have a friend with an external locus of control. When my job was eliminated at my former employer, I didn't hesitate to seek work in other departments that were growing.

Unfortunately, as I mentioned earlier, my friend didn't see it that way. He told me our employer didn't want any of the people who were laid off. I told him that wasn't my

---

[20] Fournier, Gillian. "Locus of Control." PsychCentral.
https://psychcentral.com/encyclopedia/locus-of-control/ (accessed October 8, 2017).

experience or the experience of a mutual friend, but it didn't seem to make any difference.

It was 2011 when I had that conversation. I believe it took my friend between two to four years to land a position. I landed my position in less than six months.

If you are uncertain which perspective is best for you, consider these findings shared by Peter Baskerville:

Research shows that people with an internal locus of control are more inclined to be better off, more achievement oriented and hold better paying jobs. These folks also tend to be physically healthier, happier, and more independent. In addition, they are not as likely to be swayed by the opinions of others.[21]

Peter Baskerville also recommends meditating on this quote from Carl Jung.

I am not what happened to me, I am what I choose to become.

Knowing Yourself

Successful job seeking requires knowing our unique strengths and weaknesses. Recently, I realized that sometimes when I am stressed, my ability to think clearly can drop to 50% of what it normally is.

I also realized I can take action to minimize stress's impact. Because of the impact stress can have on my performance, I need to be sensitive to how I feel. If I feel stressed, I take ten long, deep breaths. If I still feel stressed, I go for a fifteen-minute walk.

Do you have unique strengths and weaknesses requiring special strategies like these?

Your World View

I'll never forget waiting for a seminar with the excellent outplacement firm, Lee Hecht Harrison. I heard someone make a negative, pessimistic comment. I don't remember what she said, but it stuck with me. My immediate thought was:

---

[21] Baskerville, Peter. "How do I stay positive? And why?" Quora. https://www.quora.com/How-do-I-stay-positive-And-why (accessed October 8, 2017).

That's why she was laid off. Bosses can't stand negativism. It undermines morale and makes people not even want to try.

Olivia and Kevin, the good folks at Career Attraction, say it best:

There are two ways to look at life, your job search and the inevitable interviewing rejection each job seeker incurs.

The first is to imagine the worst and be prone to depression...the second is to look at interviewing rejection as a temporary setback and leverage that disappointment into action rather than stagnation.

Job seekers who think positively will interview more effectively, receive higher salaries and enjoy more career options.[22]

If you'd like to find out more, read Olivia and Kevin's post, "Why Optimistic Jobseekers Do Better and How To Become One."

They have a lot of great information about changing the way you think and changing the way you interview.

Your Beliefs

When it comes to job seeking, I like what Saint Augustine said:

Pray as though everything depended on God. Work as though everything depended on you.

Because I follow this strategy, I believe I will be hired.

I also believe I'll be hired, since my last employer gave me more chances to learn how to get hired than most people have in their lifetime. Because of those experiences:

I realize I must stand out from all of the other candidates.

I stand out by clearly communicating my track record of solving complex problems.

The best way to communicate how you can solve problems is to include your stories of overcoming obstacles and resolving work issues in:

- Your Cover Letter

---

[22] Gamber, Olivia & Kevin Kermes. "Why optimistic job seekers do better and how to become one." Career Attraction. http://www.careerattraction.com/why-optimistics-job-seekers-do-better-and-how-to-become-one/ (accessed October 8, 2017).

- Your Resume
- Your Achievement Stories
- Your LinkedIn Recommendations
- Your Portfolio.

The Impact of Others' Opinions

Sooner or later we all confront other people's opinions.

When this happens, remember what my 58 years taught me:

Not everyone will appreciate you and everything you can offer.

Many people think:

If you don't live life as I do, something is the matter with you.

We know they couldn't be more wrong.

While we're waiting for them to figure that out, don't let these people bother you.

Move on and …

… seek out those who are wise enough to truly appreciate you and all you have to offer.

Remembering that just because,

Some people don't believe in you, is no reason not to pursue your wildest dreams.

After all,

Their beliefs are just opinions, not facts.

Before Going Any Further...

Your success as a job seeker will be determined by how you make decisions.

If you make decisions based on how you feel today, you probably won't be very successful.

If instead, you make decisions based on how you will feel after the work is done, you will be successful.

I run three days a week. When I get up, I don't decide if I'm going to run based on how I feel at the moment. I decide to run based on how I will feel after my run is over.

What you'll need to accomplish, so you can successfully land a job, will require a lot from you. How will you decide what to do?

Before You Can Be Successful, You Need To Know What Failure Looks Like

One of today's best job search experts, Liz Ryan, described what failure looks like for a job seeker:

The worst -- and most common -- interview mistake you can make is to be a forgettable applicant, and to leave the building without leaving any impression whatsoever on your interviewer.

Managers are busy. They are overloaded with information the same way we all are. If you don't make your mark in your job interview, all traces of you will have left your manager's memory before you get home.[23]

Many job seekers believe they should just sit there, respond to a hiring manager's questions and then ask one or two questions at the end.

That is a recipe for failure.

---

[23] Ryan, Liz. "The Fatal Job Interview Mistake You Won't Realize You're Making." Forbes. https://www.forbes.com/sites/lizryan/2015/12/16/the-fatal-job-interview-mistake-you-wont-realize-youre-making/#27912cea3569 (accessed October 8, 2017).

Impress Hiring Managers With Your Achievement Stories

Now that you know what failure looks like, this is how you lead a lasting impression.

The hiring manager needs to know what you can do for her. She's looking for what you did, because that's the best indication of what you can do for her.

Depending on your years of experience, this can range:

— from having mastered Microsoft Excel, including pivot tables and Vlookups, to writing VBA code to automating the work of your department and reducing cycle time 80%.

— from how met your sales quota three years in a row to how you went to the Achievers Club five years in a row for exceeding quota by 25% or more, and

— from organizing an industry conference for 100 guests to organizing and running five industry conferences where attendees numbered between five and ten thousand.

Appreciating Your Work

Before you can write your Achievement Stories, you need to appreciate your achievements. You cannot take your work for granted.

Malcolm Forbes, Forbes' magazine's late publisher, said:

Too many people overvalue what they are not and undervalue what they are.

What usually happens is that if we do something, it seems commonplace, not special, just ordinary. However, when we see someone doing something we cannot do, we're impressed.

What we're not considering is whether the person who impressed you can do what you can do.

We're also not asking ourselves:

"Why did you keep your job so long?"

"Why did you get raises?"

"Why did you get promoted?"

"Why did you receive those awards?"

"Why did you get recognized as often as you did, via awards or complementary messages from your boss and others?"

If you're not getting raises, promotions, awards or complements, there could be a number of reasons. It might be that your company cannot afford to provide raises and promotions. It's possible that a boss may think that if you get awards and compliments, you'll ask for a raise, which her budget doesn't permit.

Unfortunately, there are also times when a boss may not want to draw attention to you because she's afraid of you, afraid you'll outshine her, afraid you'll get her job.

Of course, you need to be careful around someone like this.

I once gave a presentation to a group of people, including my boss and her boss. After the presentation, my boss's boss said it was excellent. All my boss did was look at me for what seemed like a long time. As long as she worked there, she never let me give another presentation.

Important Warning

Before you raise a red flag and say, "I can't do this," remember: being shy about sharing your strengths can result in not getting offers. If you get offers, they will be at lower salaries.

For example, I have a friend, who I'll call Jonathan. I coached him on the value of achievement stories. I also recommended him to a staffing firm. He told me later that they never called him back.

They never called him back, because he never spoke of his achievements.

Staffing firms are paid to provide great candidates to prospective employers. If someone can't promote themselves — if someone cannot explain why they are a great candidate — they'll never get a call back, whether it's from a staffing firm, a hiring manager, or anyone else.

While I understand that my friend probably views Achievement Stories as bragging, I overcame this hurdle. When I talk about accomplishments, I say:

"I'm blessed with the ability to…"

"I've been fortunate enough to…"

"Leadership appreciates how…"

"Co-workers appreciate how…"

This is an ideal way to communicate your achievements, because hiring managers prefer humble candidates. But they do want to hear about your achievements.

Responsibilities or Achievements?

A common belief among job seekers is, "I need to explain my responsibilities in prior roles." No. Hiring managers determine that by looking at your job title

One way to do both is to list achievements, highlighting your responsibilities. Amy Michalenko describes this excellently, when she says:

A duty describes what you did and an accomplishment describes how well you did it. For example, "planned events" would be considered a job duty, whereas "raised $100,000 by selling out tickets to a 200-person charity event" is an accomplishment.[24]

What is an Achievement Story?

As noted in the Hiring Manager's Secrets chapter, hiring managers want to know:

How you made money for your employer,

How you saved money for your employer,

How you made yourself, your department, your division, or your company more productive.[25]

They want to know how you made a positive difference. This is your time to answer the above questions with real-life examples from your experience.

According to "Ask A Manager" blogger, Alison Green, resumes that stand out tell the reader what you accomplished that someone else wouldn't have in the same position.[26]

For example, if you're like me you may have:

— trained managers to sell products through a new ordering system by documenting the process and conducting training sessions,

— took on the work of two laid off employees, or

---

[24] Michalenko, Amy. "Resume Revamp: How To Turn Your Duties Into Accomplishments." The Muse. https://www.themuse.com/advice/resume-revamp-how-to-turn-your-duties-into-accomplishments (accessed October 8, 2017).

[25] Levinson, Jay Conrad & David E. Perry. *Guerrilla Marketing for Job Hunters 3.0. Hoboken, NJ: Wiley.* 2011 p. 40.

[26] Green, Alison. *How to Get a Job.* p.14-16 The book is available at Alison's website, http://www.askamanager.org/.

— developed a budgeting system enabling managers to customize their budgets based on their unique needs.

Alison also says that the hiring manager wants to know, "Were you solely interested in producing acceptable work, or did you do an impressive job?"[27]

How To Collect Your Achievement Stories

Before we can write our Achievement Stories, we need to identify each and every one. This will take some work, but the payoff is employment and higher wages and salaries.

Because I want you to look as impressive as possible, I'm going to remind you of all of the places where your achievements can be found:

Performance Reviews

I worked at a place where, at the end of every year, my boss had to convince his peers why I should get a raise and or a bonus. As a result, my performance reviews were a great place to find achievements I might have forgotten about.

Awards

Every time you receive an award, you have evidence that you are special. Depending on the number of achievements, you might want to list your awards as achievements. Usually, the reason you received the award is an achievement.

Promotions

Getting promoted is an achievement. Your promotion says to the hiring manager, "This woman is so good that we gave her more responsibility and a higher salary."

Bosses and Coworkers

---

[27] Green.

If you're wracking your brain trying to think of achievements, consider giving a list of the achievements you've identified to bosses and co-workers. Then ask them, "What's missing? What have I left out?"

Emails

If you have access to your old emails, go through each one to see what you can find. I did this every year when my boss asked for my achievements, this gave him the ammunition he needed to negotiate for my raises. This is the ammunition you need to win over the hiring manager.

LinkedIn Recommendations

Just the other day, I was reading my LinkedIn recommendations and was reminded of an accomplishment I had not included in my LI profile or resume.

As you read each recommendation, think about the work you did with that person. It may jog your memory and help you remember things you've left out.

Identify Your Strengths With Strengths Finder 2.0

One tool that can help you remember your achievements is the 'Strengths Finder' assessment. The father of Strengths Psychology, Donald O. Clifton, Ph.D, along with Tom Rath and a team of scientists at The Gallup Organization, created StrengthsFinder. You can take this assessment by purchasing the Strengths Finder 2.0 book.[28]

The value of SF 2.0 is that it helps you understand your unique strengths. Once you have this knowledge, you can review past activities and understand what these strengths enabled you to do.

Here's what I mean, in the paragraphs below, I've listed some of the strengths identified by my Strengths Finder assessment and accomplishments where these strengths were used.

"You can see repercussions more clearly than others can."

---

[28] The link at the end of this footnote takes you to the Amazon site where you can purchase the SF 2.0 book as I did. When you purchase a new book you will receive an access code that enables you to access the online assessment. I took the test in 2013 and paid approximately $50.00 for the assessment.
https://www.amazon.com/StrengthsFinder-2-0-Tom-Rath/dp/159562015X/ref=tmm_hrd_swatch_0?_encoding=UTF8&qid=&sr=

In a prior role, I witnessed products being implemented in the sales system at breakneck speed. While quick implementation seemed good, I knew speed increased the likelihood of revenue impacting errors.

I conducted an audit and uncovered a misconfigured product. While the customer had paid for the product, the revenue had never been recognized. As a result of my work, we were able to add another $7.2 million that went straight to the bottom line.

"You automatically pinpoint trends, notice problems, or identify opportunities many people overlook."

At my former employer, leadership did not audit certain product manager decisions. On my own initiative, I instituted an auditing process. This led to the discovery that one product manager's decisions cost the company more than $5M.

"Because of your strengths, you can reconfigure factual information or data in ways that reveal trends, raise issues, identify opportunities, or offer solutions."

In a former position, product managers were responsible for driving revenue, yet there was no revenue reporting at the product level. After researching the issue, I found a report used to process monthly journal entries which when reconfigured, provided product managers with monthly product revenue.

"You entertain ideas about the best ways to…increase productivity."

A few years back, I was trained by the former Operations Manager when I took on that role. After examining the tasks, I found I could reduce the time to perform the role by 66%. As a result, I was able to tell my Director I could take on some of the responsibilities of the two managers she had to let go.

"You entertain ideas about the best ways to…solve a problem."

About twenty years ago I worked for a division where legacy systems were being replaced by a new company-wide ERP system. When I discovered no one had budgeted for training in my department, I took it upon myself to identify how to extract the data my department needed to perform its role, documented those learnings and that became the basis for a two day training class.

"Sorting through lots of information rarely intimidates you. You welcome the abundance of information. Like a detective, you sort through it and identify key pieces of evidence. Following these leads, you bring the big picture into view."

Around the same time as the introduction of the new ERP system, my boss asked me to attend a meeting with his peers and his boss. At the time, I worked in the product management group for the flagship product. I was informed that we were losing large bids and no one knew why.

After working closely with the Special Bids analysts and taking time to understand their processes, I discovered the financial data feeding the special bids system was no longer being maintained and had become erroneous.

I quickly developed a short-term special bids system using cost data blessed by Finance. The Special Bids analysts used this system until a permanent system could be developed. As a result of my work we began to win large bids again.

"Your quest to interpret events, grasp facts, or understand concepts appears limitless…Discovering new ways to use your talents energizes you."

The above strength is illustrated in two sentences from a recommendation provided by a former Director, "Dependable, versatile, responsive, analytical - these are the terms that best describe Clark. He had the skills to play in 3-4 different positions on the soccer field and was able to adapt to the unique needs of the organization."

The above strength is also illustrated in the variety of roles and tasks that you can see in my LinkedIn profile. https://www.linkedin.com/in/clarkfinnical/

Please note, I am not listing these strengths to brag. I am listing these strengths to help you see the value of taking the Strengths Finder assessment.

I've included the accomplishments where those strengths were used as an example for you to follow.

It is critical that you identify how you used your strengths in your past accomplishments. Hiring managers are going to be much more interested in the accomplishments that resulted from these strengths than a simple listing of your strengths. For hiring managers, these accomplishments prove you have these strengths.

Once you've taken these steps you will not only better understand what you can bring to a new role, you will also be better able to communicate these strengths and accomplishments to hiring managers.

Ask yourself, 'What problems did you solve?'

Remember, no one will care more and understand more about your achievements than you. Your boss may be happy, because he can brag how he hired you. Your co-workers may be happy because you've made their lives easier.

But only you will be fully familiar with your achievements and the impact they had on your department and company.

Therefore, it can be helpful to use the *problem/solution method* to identify the problems your organization faced and the solutions you developed. Here are some examples from my work history:

Problem:

No one had ever measured the financial impact of Category D transactions.

Solution:

By working with Subject Matter Experts, and persevering through all of the questions, I was able to create the first report measuring Category D Transactions. Now the leadership understands their financial impact.

Problem:

Managers need business critical data fast so they can make quick decisions.

Solution:

I documented 500 pages of job aids, enabling managers to extract data from corporate systems whenever needed.

How You Work Differently From Your Co-Workers

Another way to identify achievements is to consider how you work differently from others in your team. Here are some examples from my experience:

(1) As noted above, after being trained to take over a position, I reviewed the position's functions, determined how tasks could be batched, and developed a way to perform the function with the same or greater quality in one third of the time.

(2) In one role where I was asked to create a factory forecast, I knew I couldn't take the data I was given at face value. I understood that the new product forecast was really a justification for the R&D investment.

I knew the sales force wouldn't be fully trained and comfortable with selling the new product until six months after its introduction. I also knew that the forecasts for the other products were created in a vacuum and did not take into account the impact of a new product introduction.

After adjusting for these factors, I created a factory forecast that proved to be 29% more accurate than past forecasts.

(3) As noted above, in another position, a major company-wide system was introduced, but no one had budgeted for training people in my department. I learned how to get the information the department needed to perform its role and documented what I learned. In turn, that became the basis for a two-day training class.

How Did You Change Your Department?

What was your department like before you joined it — or even while you were there — and how did you change it?

What role did you play in making these changes?

Additional Questions to Identify Achievements

Did you find products or services that had not been billed to customers?

Did you find that your employer had been under-billing customers?

Did you make more sales for your employer?

If you took action on these or enabled others to take action, you played a part in making money for your employer.

Did you find ways to get the same supplies or services for less?

Did you negotiate and receive lower costs?

Did you find a better way to do the same thing for less?

If so, you saved money for your employer.

Did you find a way to perform the same function in less time?

Did you conduct training?

Did you create documentation?

If so, you increased productivity.

Understanding What Makes You Different

As you identify all of your achievements, you'll start to understand what makes you a valuable employee. As a result, you'll be able to answer the question, "What makes you different from everyone else?"

This is the type of question you can expect in your interview. Your ability to answer this question might just determine whether you land the job or not.

If I am asked, 'What makes me different?' One of the things I will say is, 'I enjoy mastering complex things, and I persevere until I gain this mastery.'

Capture the Quantitative Impact of Your Accomplishments

Examine everything you've done, but don't merely report what you've done. Report the quantitative impact, that is, the numbers that resulted from your achievement. That's what hiring managers care about most. For example:

When I was in school, I worked in the University's Personnel department. During my time there, the Director asked if I could explain a monthly report she received from Accounts Payable.

The report identified everything charged to Personnel. Unfortunately, neither the Director nor her team could understand what it was saying. After some analysis and research, I was able to translate the confusing report into something the Director could understand.

What I did *not* do was ask the Director and her team for the financial impact of now being able to understand the report. While what I did was a valuable story to share at my next interview, it would have meant a lot more if I'd identified the dollars saved or some other quantified impact.

As noted earlier, a few years later, I worked for a high-tech company that sold equipment to Fortune 500 firms. The company wasn't winning the large deals like they had in the past, so I was asked to investigate.

I identified the process breakdown causing the problem. I also created a short-term solution, so that the company could start winning bids again while the long-term solution was being developed.

What I did *not* do — and almost have to kick myself now for not doing — was to ask for the value of the deals we were now winning. Those $$$ would have clearly explained the positive impact of my work. It would have been a wonderful talking point in my resume.

After my job was eliminated for the second time in 13 years, I started doing a better job of quantifying the impact of my accomplishments.

How to Quantify Achievement Stories

When hiring managers, recruiters, and staffing firms see a resume or Linkedin profile or attend an interview with verbiage but no numbers, they don't know what those words mean.

In fact, they know next to nothing until you add the numbers that explain the impact of your work. Here's how you can resolve this issue.

Work With Finance

Sometimes the impact of our work is not always clear. At times like this, reaching out to one of your friends in the Finance Department can be very helpful. Finance has access to numbers that are not always readily available to other departments.

If you're no longer with the company, explain to the Finance associate that the numbers he provides could make the difference in determining whether you land another position.

Using a Range

Per Lily Zhang of the Muse, one reason job seekers avoid quantifying is not knowing the exact number. Lily suggests using a range.[29] Using my work experience, here's what that means:

Before: Chaired weekly product manager meeting.

After: Chaired weekly meeting with 7 to 12 product managers so plans could be discussed and coordinated. Confusion and rework were eliminated.

Frequency

Lily shared that one of the easiest ways to add numbers is to identify the frequency with which you perform a given task. This can help the hiring manager understand how much you can handle[30]. For example:

Before: Responded to pricing requests from the Sales Force.

After: Responded to 15 to 20 pricing requests from the Sales Force on a daily basis.

Scale

Everyone on the hiring side of the business loves when candidates provide numbers, because numbers explain the impact of what you've done.

The most meaningful numbers are those associated with making money, saving money, and driving productivity[31]. Here are a couple examples from my work experience:

Before: Reduced time to perform Operations Manager's role; after analysis showed tasks could be batched and performed at the end of the month.

After: Reduced time to perform Operations Manager role by 66%; after analysis showed tasks could be batched and performed at the end of the month. Asked Director if I could take on the responsibilities of employees who were laid off.

Before: Analysis revealed misconfigured offers; worked with other departments to correct errors. Implemented process to prevent future errors.

After: Analysis revealed misconfigured offers; worked with other departments to correct errors. Recognized $7.2M. Implemented process to prevent future errors.

[29] Zhang, Lily. "How to Quantify Your Resume Bullets (When You Don't Work With Numbers)." The Muse. https://www.themuse.com/advice/how-to-quantify-your-resume-bullets-when-you-dont-work-with-numbers (accessed October 9, 2017).
[30] Zhang.
[31] Ibid.

Excellent Resource

Katharine Hansen, Ph.D, wrote one of the best articles I've ever read about quantifying achievements. Here's the link:

https://www.livecareer.com/quintessential/quantifying-accomplishments

Katharine has also written a book on the subject, <u>You Are More Accomplished Than You Think: How to Brainstorm Your Achievements for Career and Life Success</u>

How To Write Achievement Stories

Because you're asking people to take a chance on you, you need to show them why they should take a chance.

We live in a world best summarized by the words of Grant Cardone:

Sell Or Be Sold!

Practically, everything we hear and read on TV, radio, and the internet is an attempt to sell us something.

When you find yourself in front of the hiring manager, it's essential that you sell yourself. Selling yourself means helping the hiring manager understand why she should hire you.

Hiring managers want to know how you're different from all of the other candidates. If you can't answer that question, you won't get a second interview.

After my job was eliminated in '95 and '02, I knew I had to quantify the impact of my work, so I would be ready for the next time.

As a result, I took detailed notes on everything I did that 1) earned money, 2) saved money, and 3) increased productivity.

I also took detailed notes on everything that set me apart from other candidates.

Because everyone responds well to stories, and detailed stories add to your credibility, I created Achievement Stories.

Achievement stories are also known as STAR stories. STAR is short for Situation – Task – Action – Result. Another name for Achievement stories is SOAR stories. (See explanation below.)

Situation

First, provide the context of what was happening. This is the before picture, namely what was going on at the time, before you took action.

Obstacles

These are the issues and problems which you had to overcome to be successful.

Action

This is where you explain what you did to overcome the issues and problems.

Results

This is where you share the outcome of your action – both quantitatively and qualitatively.[32]

How Achievement Stories Help You

Achievement stories are exactly what the hiring manager wants to hear, because they explain in detail what you've done in the past.

Telling the hiring manager what you've done in the past tells her what she can expect from you if she hires you.

Achievement stories are also the best way to share your accomplishments. According to a recent Harvard Business Review article:

When you want to motivate, persuade, or be remembered, start with a story of human struggle and eventual triumph. It will capture people's hearts – by first attracting their brains.[33]

Another Harvard Business Review article reminds us:

---

[32] Cattelan, Linda. "The S.O.A.R. Answer Model." HumanResources.com. http://www.humanresources.com/491/the-soar-answer-model/ (accessed October 9, 2017).

[33] Zak, Paul J. "Why Your Brain Loves Good Storytelling." Harvard Business Review. https://hbr.org/2014/10/why-your-brain-loves-good-storytelling (accessed October 9, 2017).

People are attracted to stories ... because we're social creatures and we relate to other people.[34]

Achievement Story Example #1

Here's an Achievement Story I've shared in interviews.

Situation

In my department, one of the things we did was implement products in the Sales systems.

Obstacles

I observed that speed was the top priority. I also knew that there weren't many controls in the process.

Action

Knowing that my concern alone would not change things, I started auditing the coding of every product.

Results

I uncovered a product where the customer had paid us for three years, however because the offer wasn't implemented correctly, we never recognized the revenue. Working with Finance, we were able to recognize $7.2M that year. That revenue went straight to the bottom line, because the costs had already been incurred.

The other positive outcome was people now understood this was an issue that had to be addressed. As a result, a new process was established where I had to approve the coding for the products. In addition, the focus on this error made the coding folks significantly more careful going forward.

Achievement Story Example # 2

Situation

---

[34] Monarth, Harrison. "The Irresistible Power of Storytelling as a Strategic Business Tool." Harvard Business Review. https://hbr.org/2014/03/the-irresistible-power-of-storytelling-as-a-strategic-business-tool

I joined a department of product managers who were measured on the profitability of their products. There was just one problem. There was no reporting to tell them how they were doing.

Obstacle

At the time, Finance was only interested in reporting Total Revenue. They weren't interested in reporting at the product level, which was the level of detail the product managers needed. No one was taking any action to address this issue.

Action

I did some investigating. I spoke with those folks familiar with available reporting.

Result

I discovered a report created to process journal entries. The report contained product-level detail.

Using this information, I created product level revenue reporting for many years.

As a result, the product managers could finally do their job. They could now make fact-based decisions. They could quickly see which products were succeeding and which were failing. This was a great success for the department.

More Benefits of Achievement Stories

When the hiring manager says, *"Tell me about yourself"*, I usually reply, *"One of the best ways to get to know me is for me to share an Achievement Story."*

Usually, interviewers are more than happy to let you share one story after another.

Of course, you never want to appear to be taking over the interview, so when I complete one story, I always ask if I can share another.

The average interviewer is not comfortable interviewing, so when you're sharing stories, they're off the hook, because you're filling that time.

The Many Types of Achievements

A key point that I'd like you to take away is:

There are many types of achievements.

Besides the achievements above, achievements can also include things like mastering a new software program or learning how to create a new report.

As long as you can speak about the details behind the situation, the obstacles, the actions you took and the results, you have achievements.

The bottom line is, being able to master anything will show that you're a capable person. Depending on your level of experience, you may prefer to discuss how you became an Eagle Scout or how you were able to make the varsity team.

Remember, Achievement Stories answer the question, "What can this person do?" It is essential that you give the best possible answer to this question.

How Enthusiasm Multiplies The Impact of Achievement Stories

American businessman, Paul J. Meyer, said:

Enthusiasm glows, radiates, permeates and immediately captures everyone's interest.

Because I've enjoyed the work I've done and I've enjoyed solving these problems, my enthusiasm captures everyone's interest.

When the hiring manager sees your enthusiasm, she'll like the fact that you are excited about your work. She'll also find you hard to forget.

I brought 17 Achievement stories to my last interview. I'm not saying that I had the chance to share them all, but I did share many of them.

I also took hard copies of my achievement stories, so that I could refer to them in the interview. I later offered these hard copies to the hiring manager.

Where Are Achievement Stories Used?

Achievement stories are used in your resume, your LinkedIn profile, and your interviews:

In your resume, your achievements will be bulleted sentences.

In your LinkedIn profile, it will be a more detailed paragraph.

In your interviews, achievement stories enable the hiring manager to understand your accomplishments in detail.

They are also great additions to your cover letter and portfolio.

What If I Don't Want To Brag?

I've mentioned this before and I'll mention it again because it is critical…

Before you raise a red flag and say, "I can't do this," remember: being shy about sharing your strengths can result in not getting offers. If you do get offers, chances are they will be at lower salaries.

I have a friend who I'll call Jonathan. I coached him on the importance and value of achievement stories. I also recommended him to a staffing firm

He told me later that after his interview, the staffing firm never called him back. They never called him back, because he never spoke of his achievements.

Staffing firms are paid for providing great candidates to prospective employers. If someone can't promote themselves — if someone cannot explain why they are a great candidate — they'll never get a call back, whether it's from a staffing firm, a hiring manager or anyone.

While I understand that my friend probably views Achievement Stories as bragging, I overcame this hurdle by describing my accomplishments this way:

"I'm blessed with the ability to…"

"I've been fortunate enough to…"

"Leadership appreciates how…"

"Co-workers appreciate how…"

This is an ideal way to communicate your achievements because hiring managers prefer humble candidates.

Networking

Networking Defined

Some Job Search experts' networking advice is limited to the words, "Go network." This isn't very helpful, particularly for those of us who are more introverted than others.

I'd like to make up for their shortcomings.

Networking is

Friends helping friends

Think about it this way: almost everyone has lost a job at least once or knows someone who has lost a job. So, we've either felt each other's pain or have been close to it.

As a result, almost everyone will want to help you connect with the right person, <u>if you don't make it too hard for them.</u>

Successfully Starting A Networking Conversation

Effective networking begins with small talk, and in a recent article, Drake Baer lays out a networking strategy this introvert never considered.

Drake says that the French are better conversationalists, because talking about work is inappropriate in France. More importantly, the French view jobs as boring. There are other things they'd rather talk about.

The French like ice-breakers that ask where people are from or where they like to vacation.

While Drake acknowledges that asking someone about their work can provide a better understanding of that person's way of life, he realizes it can also be viewed as a way to assess someone's financial status.

This point reminded me of a conversation I had with someone whose child had learning difficulties. In the course of our conversation, I asked the father what he did, and he replied that he worked at a local hospital.

Being familiar with his son's school, I knew that the father must have been either a doctor or a highly paid administrator.

To Drake's point, the father was more comfortable not revealing his status.

Drake reminds us the goal of small talk is *the association between people* more than *the communication of ideas*.

The point isn't to wow another person but to get to know the other person. In other words, "relationships start by relating."

Drake hits the nail on the head when he says, 'What's important is beginning your conversation with something both of you experienced, such as the traffic', "The Walking Dead," Sunday Night Football, or "The Big Bang Theory."

Drake brings it all together when he says, by taking these steps, "You draw a verbal triangle between you, the other person, and some third conversational thing."[35]

Drake ends his post by talking about a close friend who'd read the same research. His friend went to a college buddy's wedding where he only knew the groom. However, he was determined to "carefully associate with his fellow guests."

He patiently asked the many guests how they knew the groom and bride and what he found was, "it's not about what you do, but what you have, as the saying goes, in common."[36]

The Rewards of Small Talk

One of the individuals Drake quotes is David Roberts. David wrote an article entitled, "Why Small Talk Is So Excruciating." In the article, he gives all introverts, myself included, something to consider the next time we criticize small talk:

Most people feel the need to get comfortable with one another before they jump into the deep end of serious conversation or ongoing friendship.

Which means if you hate and avoid small talk, you are also, as a practical matter, cutting yourself off from lots of meaningful social interaction, which is a bummer.

Also, research shows that more frequent small talk, even among those who identify as introverts, makes people happier.[37]

In other words, if you want to be comfortable with people and if you want to be happier, practice small talk as often as possible.

---

[35] Baer, Drake. "Why The French Are Better At Small Talk Than Americans." ThriveGlobal. https://www.thriveglobal.com/stories/10798-why-the-french-are-better-at-small-talk-than-americans (accessed October 9, 2017).

[36] Baer.

[37] Roberts, David. "Why small talk is so excruciating." Vox. https://www.vox.com/2015/7/7/8903123/small-talk (accessed October 9, 2017).

Almost Everyone Is Open To Talking

One of the other stumbling blocks to successful small talk is the belief that no one wants to talk with us.

Recently, Nicholas Epley, a University of Chicago psychologist, noticed the antisocial behavior of passengers on his commuter train and decided to conduct experiments.

When he asked about initiating a conversation, his fellow travelers rated the difficulty of breaking the ice at a four on a scale of zero to six. They also guessed fewer than half of their targets would want to talk.

Interestingly, their beliefs ran counter to the first experiment's results, for no one was rebuffed.

In other words, the risk of saying 'Hi' is approximately zero.

Nicholas attributes these perceptions to the belief that everyone is willing to talk, but thinks everyone else is unwilling. There could be a train full of people who want to strike up a conversation, but it remains silent nonetheless.[38]

The H.E.R. Method

When attending an event with many people, Danielle D. Dupree suggests you stop waiting to be introduced. Instead, introduce yourself to someone who looks as awkward as you feel.[39]

Danielle recommends the H.E.R. method.

H is for Hobbies.

E is for Excited About.

R is for Relationships.

Danielle suggests these questions to start conversations:

"What do you do when you're not working?"

---

[38] Hutson, Matthew. "Why New Yorkers — and Everyone Else — Should Pursue Small Talk More." NYMag.com. http://nymag.com/scienceofus/2014/07/why-new-yorkers-should-small-talk-more.html (accessed October 9,2017).

[39] Dupree, Danielle D. "The Introvert's Guide To Meeting Strangers Without Feeling Fake Or Awkward." LinkedIn. https://www.linkedin.com/pulse/introverts-guide-meeting-strangers-without-feeling-fake-dupree (accessed October 9,2017).

"What are you excited about?"

"Who else do you know attending this conference?"

After they answer, ask yourself, "*How can I help this person? Who can I connect them with?*"

If they name someone, say something like, "*Oh cool! How'd you guys meet?*" If they name no one, make them your new best friend.

Per Danielle, the H.E.R. method works, because it shows that you're interested in them, which makes them interested in you.

In addition, with the H.E.R. method, there's no need to avoid or fear small talk.[40]

I stated at the beginning almost everyone will want to help you connect with the right person, <u>if you don't make it too hard on them.</u>

Once you've had an opportunity to connect and establish a relationship, that is the time to say, "I'm looking for introductions to people who work for these two companies. Do you know someone? If not, do you know someone who might know the right person?"

Don't Forget These People In Your Network

One thing that we're all guilty of, myself included, is underestimating the size of our network.

Here is some helpful info from the HelpGuide.org to remind us how many different people are actually in our network:

You already belong to many networks (family, friends, colleagues, fellow civic club members, etc.), and your job search network can be a natural outgrowth of these contacts.

Each network connects you to another network (for example, your child's teacher can connect you with other parents, schools, and school suppliers). And each member of your network may know of an available job or a connection to someone who will know of one.

Identify Your Networking Opportunities

Using myself as an example, I decided to identify the number of people I could speak to. I identified:

---

[40] DuPree.

25 Family members,

35 people at church,

12 teachers at my son's and daughter's schools,

12 parents of my son's and daughter's friends,

30 people I went to high school with, and

10 people I went to college with.

All in all, this amounts to 120+ individuals who may know people at companies where I work or may know others who may know.

This is *before* I count co-workers and bosses from prior roles.

This also excludes people who've provided LinkedIn recommendations.

Of course, that doesn't even begin to include the people in line with you at the grocery store, the gym, the DMV, the restaurant, etc.

Give yourself a minimum daily quota of 5 people to contact. Even if these folks don't live in your hometown, you never know if they know folks who live near you.

Networking's Many Forms

Networking can take many forms. For example:

Exchange Favors: During the great recession, Tom Konger reached out and requested a LinkedIn recommendation. After he helped me remember who he was and how we worked together, I was more than happy to give him a great recommendation.

Three years later, I relocated to Tom's stomping grounds and was looking for work. Tom's employer had an open position where I was a great match. Tom put in a good word for me with the hiring manager. I interviewed, and because of Tom's support I was in the running for that role for a number of months, in spite of the automated rejection letter from the HR system.

Share Valuable Information: Kari Maribal says that when valuable information comes your way — even if it is of no value to you — share it with your network.

Every time I see open positions I share them with my network. According to Kari, sharing valuable information can reinforce your connections and show you are a valuable resource. [41]

---

[41] Mirabal, Kari. "'Pause Before You Pass' & Maximize Networking." Kari. http://karimirabal.com/blog/pause-pass-maximize-networking/ (accessed October 9, 2017).

Networking Events: I've attended a variety of networking events, including an event advertised on LinkedIn. I came to realize that the Financial Planner who organizes these events does it to drive customers to his business. Nothing ever came of that event.

Finding Networking Events Worth Going To

Find local networking opportunities by entering search terms, like you see below, in the Google search bar.

"networking" Tampa OR Clearwater OR "St. Petersburg"

I've found its best to put quotation marks around networking otherwise it returns every reference to "network".

When the results are returned <u>click "Tools." > change "Any time" to "Past Year" > change "Sort by relevance" to "Sort by date."</u> After I chose "Sort by date," there was a lot to sort through. Some of the sites returned were,

- "The Network in Tampa, A Business and Social Networking Event"

- "The Upper Tampa Bay Chamber of Commerce" site mentioned that it sponsors three separate regularly scheduled networking events.

- The Power Broker Magazine contained a link to a Startup Networking event.

- "weconnect's Tampa Startup and Tech Networking Mixer powered by Google."

- A local site specializing in top things to do in Tampa Bay included a networking opportunity geared to Latin connexions (their word.)

- A link to a local radio station and its networking link returned this treasure,

    o a Career Fair, Healthcare conference, monthly open networking meeting, Association of Food Equipment Manufacturers conference, IT Industry conference, Amusements and Attractions Industry conference and a Shippers conference.

Eventbrite.com can also help you find networking events. Go to Eventbrite.com, enter your city and press search. Next select, Networking event type. A few clicks revealed these events:

- Disrupt Tampa

- Network After Work Tampa at the Tampa Club

- Tampa Career Fair

- The CEO Forum – Tampa Bay

Of course, LinkedIn provides an endless source of networking opportunities via its many groups. Simply enter "Networking" in the search bar, and then select Groups.

A great way to identify some of these groups is to enter 'networking' in the search bar at the top of the LinkedIn page and select groups. This will return those groups containing 'networking' in their Group name.

If you are interested in networking "meetup" groups, enter these search terms in the Google search bar for your community:

Meetup "networking" Tampa OR Clearwater OR "St. Petersburg"

The Value of Weak Ties

In 1973, sociologist Mark Granovetter asked professionals how they landed their new job. Almost 28% found their jobs through an individual they saw only occasionally or rarely. That is why they are called "weak ties."[42]

Granovetter explains that your good friends tend to be from the same background. As a result, your friends know what you know.

Weak ties, however, are not from the same background. Therefore, it is much more likely a weak tie will know about a new job opportunity you've never heard of.[43]

Identifying Weak Ties

---

[42] "The real way to build a social network." Fortune. http://fortune.com/2012/01/24/the-real-way-to-build-a-social-network/ (accessed October 9, 2017).
[43] Fortune.

80

Marc Miller of Next Avenue has a great plan to identify your weak ties. Specifically, build lists of people you have worked with over the last 20 years.

The first group includes people who worked in the same function as you (HR, Engineering, Programming, Sales, etc.)

The second group includes people who worked in a different function.

Use LinkedIn's Advanced Search to answer these questions:

If people worked in the same function as you, who are they working for? Did they change functional areas? If so, reach out and ask them how they did it.

If people worked in a different function, where do they work now? Have they changed industries? If they did, ask them how they did it.[44]

Next, reach out to these folks and ask:

Do they like their current employer?

Can they recommend other companies worth checking out?[45]

Could they introduce you to anyone at their current company or at another company?

[44] Miller, Marc. "To Get A Job, Use Your Weak Ties." Forbes. https://www.forbes.com/sites/nextavenue/2016/08/17/to-get-a-job-use-your-weak-ties/#1c85f2766b87 (accessed October 9, 2017).
[45] Miller.

Will Spelling Keep You Out Of Interviews?

Whether we like it or not, hiring managers judge job seekers based on how our resumes, cover letters, and LinkedIn profiles are written.

That's why it is essential that you turn on Microsoft Word's spell-check so it catches every error in your resume and cover letter.

But don't stop there, after turning on Microsoft Word's spell check, <u>copy all of the verbiage</u> in your LinkedIn profile and paste it into a Word document.

Here are some of the reasons I say this…

- 5,908 LinkedIn Profiles contained "Universiry" where they meant to write "University".

- 34,254 profiles contain "Graduat" where they meant to write "Graduate".

- 25 English teacher's profiles contain "Colege" where they meant to write "College".

If you're not getting interviews, take a second look at your resume, cover letter and LinkedIn profiles.

Hiring managers get to choose who they want to hire. Don't let your spelling be the reason they don't hire you.

Your Resume

Create A Winning Resume

Remember when you went car shopping, and all of the cars had a sticker in their window, listing all of their features. You need to create one of those.

You need to create a list of your features. Another name for your list of features is your resume. Your LinkedIn profile also lists your features, but we're going to talk about your resume here.

Instead of just showing you a completed resume, I thought it would help if we went over what a resume does, part by part.

The Header

Your header is important, because it's the first thing people see on your resume. You want to win them over from the start. You want to attract people, not scare them away. Your resume needs to look professional.

Whether you center your heading, left align it, or align it to the right, it needs to appear balanced or at least properly aligned. If it isn't, it could turn off people simply because it doesn't look right.

Check out the header in the resume below. While you want to make your name larger than the rest of the header, don't make it too large. The name in the heading is Helvetica Bold 16 font. Don't go any larger than a Helvetica 20 font.

Some people might think a large font means a large ego. You don't want to send that message.

The rest of the header is Helvetica Bold 11 font.

Justin Tyme

1262 Main Street, Spring Garden, PA

Home 555-555-5555   ltyme@gmail.com   Cell 666-666-6666|

SUMMARY

I am a Finance Operations Analyst who quickly masters my role, becomes your trusted advisor, makes the complex simple and resolves your most challenging problems. I'm commended because I added $8M to the bottom line, cut the time to perform my role by 50% and successfully implemented three corporate-driven IT projects.

Analysis/Operations/Reporting	Training/Documentation
Project Management/Teaming	Six Sigma Lean Black Belt

WORK EXPERIENCE

ABCCO, Senior Manager   XXXX-XXXX
Developed fiscal year plans for the team. Forecast quarterly expenses with 97% accuracy.

- Reduced cycle time to perform Senior Manager role by 50%.
- Grow open rates 200% for Business-2-Business mailers by researching best practices and implementing new subject lines and send times.
- Maximized impact of the Marketing team by ensuring that 99-100% of all funds were used for new programs.
- Recognized 1000 employees for exemplary service by project managing Award program, which enabled customers to recognize employees.

ABCCO, Operations Analyst   XXXX-XXXX
Drove three corporate initiatives and their IT projects to closure, supported Six Sigma and Kaizen programs, identified and implemented new practices and processes for ending product support on legacy equipment, created business process improvements.

- Added $5M to the bottom line and preserved $8M by analyzing offer creation and sunset processes and implementing corrective measures.
- Generated $3M in billings by leading cross functional initiative to correct under-billing of 5000 customers while reducing billing failure rate by > 50%.
- Project managed development / delivery of training materials for new Indian team while interviewing job applicants, providing on-site training and on-going mentoring.
- Created new reporting leading to improved decision-making: Operations Review highlighting financial and operations results for executives, Monthly Portfolio Revenue reports for Offer Managers and maintenance contract reports.
- Enhanced Associate productivity by documenting 750 pages of job aids explaining how to create reports by retrieving business critical data from Business Objects and other systems.

Contact Info

Work Experience

Education / Awards

Skills / Training

Certifications

JUSTIN TYME (215.555.1212)   PAGE 2

ABCCO, Auditor / Program Manager   XXXX-XXXX
Conducted win/loss analysis, special bid support, pricing support for enterprise server product line, and transition of business results and planning activities from legacy systems to Business Objects.

- Performed full value stream analysis of competitive bids process after successive competitive losses. Found erroneous cost data in special bids system. Created special bids tool with accurate cost data resulting in competitive pricing and increased sales.
- Created offer reporting enabling Leadership to see all non-switch equipment and corresponding revenue driven by every switch sale.
- Documented Business Objects job aids and developed two-day Business Objects training class when no training was budgeted.

ABCCO, Planning Analyst   XXXX-XXXX
Developed unit, revenue and market share plan, interlocked with sales, forecasted results.

- Analyzed data and improved factory forecast accuracy 31%.
- Developed business plans with market leadership scenarios in revenue & market share.

ABCCO Ventures, Senior Analyst   XXXX-XXXX
Supported Sales in development of annual plans. Reported Sales results.

- Devised Field Sales budgeting program enabling District Sales Managers to customize budgets based on their unique needs.

ABCCO Ventures, Analyst   XXXX-XXXX
Developed competitive pricing in response to special pricing requests.
- Enabled Product and Channel Managers to sell their Wireless products through three ordering systems by documenting the process and conducting training sessions.

EDUCATION

MBA, Accounting and Finance, Top Notch University, City, State
BA, Business Management, Top University, City, State
Black Belt, Six Sigma Lean, Top Rated University

AWARDS

Great Award; Tremendous Award; Amazing Award; Performance Award; Innovative Award; Team Award

SKILLS

Business Objects, Excel, PowerPoint, Access

Why Omitting Your Address May Be A Wise Move

As noted earlier, I never did this, but Donna Svei, the Avid Careerist, suggests skipping your home address may be a good strategy. Here's why.

As Donna points out, recruiters calculate the length of your commute. They know that people with long commutes frequently quit "because of the commute." If you quit, they don't look good, AND they have to replace you.

Therefore, resumes with addresses far from the employer often find their way into the "maybe" or "no" pile.[46]

Donna says you can avoid this problem by using your current or most recent employer's city location. For example:

The Coca-Cola Company, Atlanta, GA (if you work at HQ) or

The Coca-Cola Company, Oakland, CA (if you work in the field)

Using your employer's city places you in a large metropolitan area.

"It gives recruiters enough information to know that you're local (if you are), without sharing that you're not local enough (if you aren't)." [47]

Your Address and Relocation

Applying for work when you live somewhere else is one of the more complex things you will do in life. I did this four years ago and I was not taken seriously until I relocated.

When you put yourselves in the employer's shoes, it's easy to understand. They don't want to invest their precious time in someone who might relocate. They have a position to fill, and they want to fill that position with someone who lives nearby.

If you'd like more information about relocation, check out these articles:

http://www.forbes.com/sites/lizryan/2015/07/10/how-to-job-hunt-when-youre-trying-to-relocate/ - 7c025e7119dc

http://careersidekick.com/applying-for-jobs-out-of-state-this-resume-tip-can-help/

Your Address and Identify Theft

More and more professionals are removing their street addresses, regardless of their target location.

If you're searching for a position in your current location and want employers to know you're a local candidate, include your city and state. However, leave your street address off to protect yourself from possible identity theft.[48]

---

[46] Svei.

[47] Ibid.

[48] Ibid.

More reasons to omit your address

Here are additional reasons why skipping your street address may be best:

I have read how some recruiters use Google Maps to get additional information on the candidate's neighborhood to help them determine the type of offer to give.[49]

Worse, if the neighborhood is ritzy, they may eliminate you because they believe the job won't pay enough for your lifestyle.

The other thing to consider is: "Do you want a hiring manager to decide whether you should be hired based on how you maintain your lawn?"

Before you think I've gone off the deep end with my above question, read this story:

One corporate president has the receptionist look in the candidate's car to see if it was neat and clean. It turns out he considers the cleanliness of the car an indicator of the candidate's character. [50]

Another reason to omit your street address is personal safety. You don't want to post a resume online where a stalker could read it.

Your Reach Number

The more phone numbers you introduce into the mix, the easier it is to miss an important message. Avoid confusion by listing one phone number, preferably the number for your cell phone — where you control the voicemail, who picks up the phone, and when.[51]

What Message Is Your Email Sending?

---

[49] Can I omit my street address from my resume without hurting my job prospects? Quora. https://www.quora.com/Can-I-omit-my-street-address-from-my-resume-without-hurting-my-job-prospects (accessed October 9, 2017).

[50] "Hiring Tricks that Job Seekers Must Know." LiveCareer https://www.livecareer.com/career-tips/on-the-job/hiring-tricks (accessed October 9, 2017).

[51] Augustine, Amanda. "16 Things You Should Remove From Your Resume." The Ladders. https://www.theladders.com/career-advice/things-you-should-never-put-on-your-resume/ (accessed October 9, 2017).

The email is one of the most overlooked parts of your resume.

Your email can hurt you or help you, so it's important to be careful when choosing the email that will go in the header of your resume. You want it to communicate the right message.

I say this, because most people don't give a second thought to their email. It's something they created years ago, and they view it as a part of their identity.

As a natural but often unfortunate consequence, most people don't realize how others might view their email.

Here are some emails that could hurt you:

<u>WilburSmith1950@gmail.com</u>

Year of birth: Avoid using what could be interpreted as the year of your birth. You might make the reader think you're too qualified or not qualified enough for the role they're looking to fill. [52]

<u>JesusisLord@gmail.com</u>

Religion: Don't talk about it; UNLESS you want to work at a church, synagogue, mosque, etc.[53]

<u>Trumpin2016@gmail.com</u>

Politics: Like religion, there are few things better at turning off people.

<u>RavensForever@gmail.com</u>

Sports teams: If the hiring manager is upset at how your team beat his team, do you think you'll have a chance?[54]

<u>binkypoo@yahoo.com</u>

Or

<u>PartyAnimal@gmail.com</u>

Unprofessional emails: Cute is great when messaging your friends and family, but it sends the wrong message in a business setting. It says, "I'm not a professional person. I don't act like a professional, especially publicly. So, I could be an embarrassment if you hire me".[55]

---

[52] "Your job search toolkit – Part Three: E-mail addresses . . . what's in a name? You'd be surprised!" Plan B Communications. http://www.planbcomms.com/PlanBCommsBlog/?p=123 (accessed October 10, 2017).
[53] N., Stephanie. "Why recruiters care about your email address." Snagajob.com. http://www.snagajob.com/resources/why-recruiters-care-about-your-email-address/ (accessed October 10, 2017).
[54] Plan B Communications.
[55] Yate, Martin. "4 Killer Tactics to Get Your Email and Resume Read." Job-hunt.org.

OrvilleJones@aol.com

Sending the wrong message: AOL started in 1992. To quote Chameleon Resumes:

"By having an aol.com address, you could be subliminally communicating that you probably have at least 20+ years experience (even if you have not been on AOL that long), resistant to change (especially if you actually have been using AOL email that long), and possibly a technophobe." [56]

You don't want to create this type of impression. I read an article in CIO magazine recently where a hiring manager said, "We would never consider someone for an IT job if they had an aol.com email."

Chameleon even says that using hotmail.com or yahoo.com in a resume with just duties or an older style format could lead people to think your skills are not up to date. [57]

TheTenOfUs@gmail.com

A family email: This email may make a hiring manager wonder if you'll get the office sick when the flu is going around. She also might wonder whether you'll ever get their email, since your thirteen-year-old also accesses your account. [58]

Here are some emails that can help you send the right message:

SStephens@stanford.edu

Top-tier university: If you went to a prestigious university, say so in the heading. Don't assume that hiring managers will read your entire resume, including the Education section. People are busy. [59]

TopAccountant10020@gmail.com

Or

SystemAnalyst302@gmail.com

Brand yourself: JobHunt.org says that using a 'profession centered' email introduces you as a professional. By using your profession in your email, you're saying, "I love what I do."

Since you won't be the first to have chosen "TopAccountant" or "SystemAnalyst," use your zip code or area code when creating the email address. [60]

http://www.job-hunt.org/resumes/killer-tactics-to-get-your-resume-read.shtml (accessed October 10, 2017).

[56] Rangel, Lisa. "How to Make Your Email Address Work (And Not Work) for You." Chameleon Resumes. http://chameleonresumes.com/2011/07/25/how-to-make-your-email-address-work-and-not-work-for-you/ (accessed October 10, 2017).

[57] Rangel.

[58] Plan B Communications.

[59] Rangel.

[60] Yate.

Professional: Nothing is more professional than a straight-forward, no-nonsense email like the above. You can't go wrong with it.

Create A Summary That Quickly Shows What You Have To Offer

SUMMARY

I am a Financial Analyst who quickly masters my role, becomes your trusted advisor, makes the complex simple and resolves your most challenging problems. I'm commended because I added $10M to the bottom line, cut the time to perform my role by 66% and successfully implemented three corporate-driven IT projects.

As you can see in the insert above, the Summary introduces you to the reader. It begins with your title and then shares your strengths.

A Summary is used for many reasons.

People are busier than ever, and they don't want to search through your resume for your strengths.

A resume with a Summary shows that you're trying to make their job easier.

Unlike an objective, which can be interpreted as, "This is what I want," a Summary communicates, "This is what I have to offer."

Communicating "This is what I have to offer" versus "This is what I want" goes over much better with hiring managers.

When you create your Summary, use the Summary earlier in this chapter as a model.

Introduce yourself using the title of the position you're applying for, then start adding strengths.s

In this example, the first sentence says:

Quickly master my role.

Become your trusted advisor.

Make the complex simple.

Resolve your most challenging problems.

The Summary goes on to list additional strengths:

Added $10M to the bottom line.

Cut the time to perform the role by 66%.

Successfully implemented three corporate-driven IT projects.

The Summary contains seven strengths and accomplishments. This gets people's attention.

In addition, the phrase, "I'm commended because," means that I'm not tooting my own horn — someone else is. This communicates humility, which is very appealing to hiring managers.

Between the Summary and Work Experience

Because the white space between the Summary and your Work Experience is one of the first things readers look at, add additional strengths for everyone to see.

List strengths not mentioned in the Summary — for example:

Analysis/Operations/Reporting   Training/Documentation

Project Management/Teaming   Six Sigma Lean Green Belt

At the same time, ensure that there's enough white space to make them stand out.

Also, don't place these words in the resume by using tables or graphics.

Applicant Tracking Systems (or ATS systems, as they are called) can't read graphics, and they misread tables.

The last thing you want to do is cause the ATS to ignore everything below your Summary. This could cause the ATS to eliminate you from consideration. (More about this important topic later.)

Instead, press the tab key to get to the correct location to enter your strengths.

Accomplishments Create A Strong Work Experience

When listing your jobs, put them under the heading, "Work Experience."

Labeling jobs "Professional Experience" or "Career Achievements" or something similar can cause the ATS to never read your "Work Experience," because it wasn't labeled "Work Experience".[61]

---

[61] Levinson, Meridith. "5 Insider Secrets for Beating Applicant Tracking Systems (ATS)." CIO. http://www.cio.com/article/2398753/careers-staffing-insider-secrets-for-beating-appli/careers-staffing/5-insider-secrets-for-beating-applicant-tracking-

List each position in this order: 1) employer's name, 2) your title, and 3) the years you worked there.

Applicant tracking systems look for company names first.[62]

Years vs. Months in Work History

Your Work Experience should be listed in years, not years and months. Here's why I say this.

At one point in my career, I was laid off in October and did not land a position until the following April. Which do you think looks better on my resume:

A) a position that ends October 2010 and a new position that begins April 2011, or

B) a position that ends in 2010 followed by a new position that begins in 2011?

If the hiring manager sees that you were unemployed, it raises questions in the hiring manager's mind. Why was he unemployed? Is something the matter with him? Don't put yourself in that position.

Add Your Accomplishments to Your Work Experience

Each position is an opportunity to communicate what you've accomplished in the role. When you review the bullets listed in the resume above, you will see that each bullet contains accomplishments.

Start Accomplishments with Action Verbs

Lastly, every bullet of your resume must begin with action verbs such as "Created," "Developed," "Achieved," etc. Use different action verbs for each bullet, because repeating the same action verb bores the reader. It also makes you look like a slacker.

I've found it helpful to consult lists of action verbs on the Internet. Here are three good sources. Thank you Wake Forest University, the University of Northern Iowa, and The Muse for making these lists available to job-seekers:

http://career.opcd.wfu.edu/files/2011/05/Action-Verbs-for-Resumes.pdf

---

systems.html?page=2 (accessed October 10, 2017).
[62] Levinson.

https://www.themuse.com/advice/185-powerful-verbs-that-will-make-your-resume-awesome

http://www.uni.edu/careerservices/students/rcl/docs/actionverbs.pdf.

Older Positions

When you get to your older (10 to 20+ year-old) positions, strongly consider combining them. The older they are, the less interesting they are to the hiring manager.

Include accomplishments with these positions but significantly less accomplishments than your most recent jobs.

For example, in a recent role, I used five bullets, each with multiple lines as well as three lines of accomplishments above the bullets.

In older roles, which will be significantly less important to a hiring manager, I combined roles.

For example, my resume has two positions from 1989 to 1995. This is actually a combination of four to five roles.

Unlike the recent role, I had only one line of accomplishments above the bullets. I also used only one bullet for each position.

Short-Term Jobs

If you worked at a (non-temporary) job for only a few months, it may be best to remove it from your resume.

Leaving a short-lived job or two off your resume shouldn't hurt, as long as you're open about your experience if asked in an interview. [63]

Employment Gaps

One of the reasons I recommend using *years* in your resume instead of *months and years* is that it hides those months when you weren't working.

Would you rather have a resume showing:

a job ending February 2010 and your next job starting November 2011, or

a job ending in 2010 and your next job starting in 2011?

---

[63] Greenawald, Erin. "43 Resume Tips That Will Help You Get Hired." The Muse. https://www.themuse.com/advice/43-resume-tips-that-will-help-you-get-hired (accessed October 10, 2017).

If you can't land a job, there are things you can do that create a positive story. For example:

In 2010 when my job search was taking longer than it had in the past, I decided to pursue a Six Sigma Lean Green Belt through Villanova University's online program. That impressed the hiring manager who eventually hired me.

I worked with someone recently who invested her time and money to become MS Office Certified while out of work. She also pursued a highly sought-after industry certification.

A friend uses the title, "Child Care Specialist" to describe the period of her life when she was home with her kids. She also recruited and managed a group of people who sold Longaberger baskets as part of a successful MLM group.

Caregiver

When we're not taking care of our children, we sometimes need to care for our parents or other loved ones.

A recent Pongo post discusses two ways to list this time in your resume. One way is to be concise and to the point:

Leave of Absence   2004 - 2006
Full-time caregiver during family member's illness.

Pongo (https://www.pongoresume.com/) suggests that you mention this period in one sentence in the interview, immediately state your readiness to return to a professional role, and then state that your strengths are a great match for the position.

Pongo then suggests redirecting the conversation so the hiring manager focuses on your strengths. Here is their advice verbatim:

"During my leave of absence in 2004 to 2006, I was caring for a close family member during a serious illness. Now, I'm ready to return to a professional role, and I think my qualifications will fit well in the _____ position."

Then, you can change the subject by asking a question such as, "What was it about my background that caught your eye?"[64]

If you are in a healthcare field, Pongo suggests using this experience to demonstrate your qualifications for a position in healthcare. Here is their recommendation:

---

[64] "Has Caring for a Loved One Left a Gap In Your Resume?" Pongo. https://www.pongoresume.com/blogPosts/291/has-caring-for-a-loved-one-left-a-gap-in-your-resume-.cfm (accessed October 10, 2017).

Full-Time Caregiver   2004 - 2006

Provided round-the-clock care for seriously ill family member, including medication management, assistance with activities of daily living, coordinating in-home therapies and services, and therapeutic recreation.

In the Interview:

"Between 2004 and 2006, I was caring for [a close family member/my mother/my father/my spouse] at the end of [his/her] life. I was fortunate to have the health care skills to be effective in that difficult role."

Then, you can change the subject by asking a question such as, "Can you tell me what you consider to be the most important qualities to be successful in the _____ role?"[65]

Volunteering

Volunteering can be a great way to: 1) demonstrate your skills and 2) show how you are giving back to society.

Make sure you capture all of your achievements and strengths, and don't sell yourself short.

Susan Ellis says that the title "Volunteer" should not be used, because it does not communicate the work you accomplished.

She goes on to say that, if you tutored, use the title "Tutor." If you coordinated a project, use the title "Project Coordinator."[66]

Then describe your volunteer work, so that it appeals to the hiring manager. Include achievements that emphasize the skills you learned and demonstrated. Did you raise funds? Did you supervise others?

Review what you learned as a volunteer and include specific accomplishments. While you don't want to overstate what you did, you do want to give yourself the credit you deserve.[67]

Remember...

When you put a bullet on your resume, you must be prepared to tell the story behind it when the hiring manager asks in your upcoming interview.

Education

---

[65] Ibid.

[66] Ellis, Susan J. "Put Volunteer Work on Your Resume." ServiceLeader.org. https://www.serviceleader.org/volunteers/resume (accessed October 10, 2017).

[67] Ibid.

While you definitely need to include college information as well as graduate school, if applicable, strongly consider including your high school if it's prestigious.

Don't hesitate to include Magna Cum Laude, Summa Cum Laude or 'Graduated with Honors' next to your degree, if applicable.

While there are differing views about listing your GPA in your resume, Monster recommends adding your GPA if you're a student or recent graduate and your GPA is 3.0 or higher.

Monster also advises recent students to list the GPA for your major if it's better than your overall GPA.[68]

List your most advanced degree first, unless another degree / certificate or classes are more important to the employer.

If you took classes at multiple colleges, only list the college you graduated from.

If you're not finished with your degree, state that you're a candidate and that your degree will be complete by 20XX.

Did You Graduate from a Prestigious University?

If you graduated from a prestigious university or one relevant to the position you're pursuing, consider listing it first —particularly, if you don't have significant accomplishments that would be more appealing to the hiring manager.

If you did not graduate college, list your high school. If you attended a prestigious high school, be sure to include it.

Graduation Dates?

There are a number of reasons why omitting graduation dates makes sense. Different hiring managers may think that you're too young or too old. Adding years can raise questions.

For example, I had a hiring manager ask me why I didn't finish my undergraduate degree in four years. Do you want to answer questions like this in your interview?

Continuing Education

---

[68] Isaacs, Kim. "How to put your education to work on your resume." Monster. http://career-advice.monster.com/resumes-cover-letters/resume-writing-tips/put-your-education-to-work/article.aspx (accessed October 10, 2017).

Don't sell yourself short by omitting additional education you've pursued since college or grad school. Employers love to see a commitment to continuous learning. This is another place you can shine.

Awards

Awards are another way to show your value; few things say more than when an employer awards you for your performance.

So, list all awards you received during your career.

Just make sure you're prepared to explain what the award is and why you received it. (Don't list the year you got the award. This can raise questions about age.)

For my interviewing process, I created a Word document listing every award and why I received it.

Keep in mind that there are some awards outside the workplace that demonstrate achievement, — such as "Eagle Scout" or military awards — which could be included here.

Skills, Certifications & Training

List all skills that will make you valuable to a potential employer.

List the skill most valuable to the employer first. Many times this will be the skill most in demand in the job market and lowest in supply.

For example, SQL skills are usually more valuable than Excel skills. Access skills are more valuable than Excel skills, unless you are adept with Excel Macros and VBA.

If you have a number of IT or other industry certifications, consider adding a separate "Certifications" section between the Education and Skills sections.

Depending on the type of position, you may want to consider listing your Skills and or Certificates before the Work Experience section.

For example, let's say you're applying for a position where a Cisco certification or other industry certificate is required. If you do not have a number of bullets demonstrating how you've applied what you learned by pursuing the Certification(s), list the Certificates first.

In addition, if you have training that doesn't fit into the above sections but will make you more appealing to an employer, by all means include a separate "Training" section.

The Length of Your Resume

The length of your resume is a function of your experience.

If you're under 30, a one page resume should be fine. As you grow older, have more roles and more achievements, a two page resume will make more sense.

Some individuals even have longer resumes but this is rare. Doctors or Academics frequently fit into this category.

Keep in mind, a hiring manager often has a large number of resumes to read. For that reason, a shorter resume — especially one focused tightly on what the hiring manager is looking for — works more in your favor.

Final Steps

Reread the resume and ask:

Does your resume make you proud of what you've done? It should.

Did you underestimate the impact of what you've done? Don't sell yourself short. Remember, this is your Sales Brochure.

Have you included all of the things that will make you appealing to a hiring manager?

Add Page 2, 3, or 4 as necessary at the top of each page. Be sure to include your name and phone number on the same line as the page number. This way, if the pages get separated, you've made it easier to find the other page — or for hiring managers to call you for the other page, if they're so inclined.

Use Microsoft Word software to do a grammar and spell check, recognizing it won't catch everything. In addition, if you misspell a word and end up spelling another word instead, spell check will not catch it.

That's why it is valuable to read through your resume. Reading it out loud will help you catch errors. Get someone else to proof it, if possible.

Consider getting a professional review after you've created your resume. This isn't always easy to do, because there are professionals who will do an excellent job and those who won't.

Here are some objective sources to consider:

1. Professionals recommended by your co-workers, friends or family.

2. Your counselor at your outplacement firm.

3. Local non-profits or government agencies whose sole purpose is to match job seekers with hiring companies. If you go to http://www.careeronestop.org/ you can search for the office closest to you.

The Resume File Name

Save your resume with a professional title such as "Joseph Smith – Marketing Director."

The naming convention is important, because when you email or upload your resume to apply for a job, the document name is visible and should not simply be "resume."

This will also help you to save the different versions of each resume that you've customized for each position.[69]

If you're emailing your resume, consider a subject line such as 'Joe Smith for Marketing Director in Houston.' [70]

~~~~~~~~~~~~~~

We all want our resumes to be read. One way to increase the likelihood of that happening is to make your resume as easy to read as possible.

Check out the next chapter to understand how to make your resume easily readable.

---

[69] Hood, Stephanie. "Confessions of a Resume Snob." LinkedIn. https://www.linkedin.com/pulse/confessions-resume-snob-stephanie-hood/ (accessed October 10, 2017).
[70] Hood.

How to Make Your Resume Easy to Read

Have you ever seen those presentations where someone decides that he needs to cram every important fact into one page — and ends up creating something that no one wanted to read? You don't want to do that.

If the recruiter or hiring manager doesn't find your resume easy to read, he's not going to waste time trying.

The Right Font

Recently, a Google recruiter shared that Google receives 3 million resumes a year. While every company isn't Google, all recruiters are busy. The last thing you want to do is give them a reason to ignore or trash your resume.

Fonts play a critical role in making your resume easy to read. Helvetica is the best font, because it's easy to read.

In a recent article, Bloomberg Business asked three "typography wonks" which fonts make a resume look classiest. Helvetica was the consensus winner.[71]

Another reason to use popular fonts like Helvetica or Arial is that the Applicant Tracking System can't read fancy fonts and will reject your resume out of confusion.[72]

In addition, Helvetica is the one resume font that is considered professional, honest, and safe.

By contrast, Times New Roman has the reputation of being staid, of communicating that you didn't think about the font you chose?[73]

White Space

In order for people to read your resume, they have to want to read it. White space, margins and multiple rows between sections can mean the difference between being read or being trashed.

Stuffing too much in too small a space will turn people off. After all, why should they struggle to read your resume when there are 100 more on their desk?

---

[71] Kitroeff, Natalie. "The Best and Worst Fonts to Use on Your Résumé." Bloomberg Businessweek. http://www.bloomberg.com/news/articles/2015-04-27/the-best-and-worst-fonts-to-use-on-your-r-sum- (accessed October 10, 2017).
[72] Slack, Mark and Erik Bowitz. "Beat the Robots: How to Get Your Resume Past the System & Into Human Hands." https://www.themuse.com/advice/beat-the-robots-how-to-get-your-resume-past-the-system-into-human-hands (accessed October 10, 2017).
[73] Kitroeff.

Remember, you don't have to cram everything in your resume on one page. If putting your information on two pages will make it easier to read and will increase its chance of getting read, wouldn't you do it?

While we need to make our resume easily readable, if it doesn't get past the Applicant Tracking System, it will never get read at all.

Read the next chapter to understand how to get through the ATS, or as some call it, the HR Elimination System.

Up To 90% of All Applications Are Rejected Before A Human Reads Them...

How To Get Through the HR Elimination System

One of the most challenging parts of job hunting in the 21st century is the Applicant Tracking System or ATS.

The ATS is something every job seeker who submits online applications has to contend with. In the pages below, I explain the ATS so that you know what you need to do to get through it.

I frequently call the ATS "The HR Elimination System."

While it is estimated the ATS eliminates 75% of the candidate pool, I've heard that in some cases, it eliminates 90% of the candidates.

You can take specific actions to reduce the likelihood of the ATS rejecting your resume.

One way is to network through friends to get an interview. If you follow this path, the ATS will not impact your job search.

For example, four years ago, a friend put in a good word for me with a hiring manager, where he worked — and I got an interview. The morning of the interview, I received an automated email from the company's ATS system, telling me I wasn't a good match for the position.

When I received the automated email, I knew there was no connection between it and my upcoming interview. When I interviewed later in the day, there was no mention of the automated email.

In other words, the Hiring Manager didn't reject me, the ATS system did.

In fact, I was in the running for the position for a number of months before it went to another candidate.

In a recent article, Lynda Spiegel shared that, not once but twice in 2013, she submitted her resume to two companies looking for a senior level human resources executive with global experience.[74]

Though Lynda's experience matched most of the requirements, within hours of hitting "send," she received emails from both companies telling her that there were other candidates more qualified for the position.[75]

Fortunately, Lynda had used her connections to send her resume to the hiring managers at both firms.

---

[74] Spiegel.
[75] Ibid.

Within one day of the ATS rejection, she received calls from both hiring managers asking her to interview, based on the strength of her resume.[76]

Avoid Rejection By The ATS System

You can also reduce the likelihood of the ATS rejecting you by following these steps:

Listing jobs under the heading, "Work Experience."

Labeling jobs "Professional Experience" or "Career Achievements" or something similar can cause the ATS to never read your "Work Experience," because it wasn't labeled as "Work Experience".[77]

When adding jobs to your resume, list your work experience in this order:

1) employer's name,

2) your title, and

3) dates you held the title.

Applicant tracking systems look for company names first.[78]

Also, use only years. No one needs to know you were out of work from June to November.

Never send your resume as a PDF. Applicant tracking systems easily misread PDF documents, because they don't know how to structure PDF documents.[79]

Don't include tables or graphics. Applicant tracking systems can't read graphics, and they misread tables.[80]

Only use commonly accepted categories. Besides "Work Experience," use "Summary," "Education," "Professional Development," "Community Involvement," etc. Straying from these phrases could result in the ATS system excluding your information.[81]

Repeat the information in the Summary section of the resume, because some ATS systems do not recognize the Summary.[82]

Use normal fonts like Helvetica or Arial — the ATS can't read fancy fonts and will reject your resume out of confusion.[83]

---

[76] Ibid.

[77] Levinson, Meridith.

[78] Ibid.

[79] Ibid.

[80] Ibid.

[81] Johnson, Kristin. "Is Your Resume ATS-Unfriendly?" Work It Daily. http://www.careerealism.com/resume-ats-unfriendly/#3WwUgH97A5oZLoi0.99 (accessed October 11, 2017).

[82] Johnson.

Use the acronym and the spelled-out form of any given title, certification, or organization. You never know whether the ATS is looking for a Certified Public Accountant or a CPA.[84]

Don't game the ATS. By "gaming the system," I'm referring to loading keywords at the end of your resume in white font or in Microsoft Word's Document Properties. Some Applicant Tracking Systems are set to omit a long list of keywords.

Some employers may view gaming the system as deceptive and will eliminate you.[85]

Cover letters count. Cover letters are also scanned along with resumes.[86]

A longer resume can help you. The length of your resume doesn't matter to an ATS. Submitting a three or four page resume enables you to add more relevant experience and keywords, which could give you a higher ranking in the system. Only do this, however, if you have work experience that fills three to four pages.[87]

The Quick Way To Customize Your Resume and Get Selected by the ATS

When I was in the job market four years ago, customizing a resume was a real pain.

It meant copying and pasting the job description into Wordle.net to identify the most commonly used words in the job description. Then I had to find the right places in my resume to insert these keywords.

Since then, I've discovered Jobscan.

If you go to https://www.jobscan.co/, you'll see what I am talking about.

When you get to the website paste your resume in the left box and paste the description of the job you're considering in the right box.

Then click Scan!

At first, Jobscan provides an overall match between the skills, keywords and education in the job description and the resume.

When I tried this the first time, the match was 56%.

---

[83] Slack.
[84] Johnson.
[85] Ibid.
[86] Slack.
[87] Ibid.

I then clicked "Next," and Jobscan told me how I did with what they call "best practices."

Jobscan gave me green check marks, because I had five or more examples of measurable results in my resume.

It also confirmed that I put the same job title in the resume as is in the job description.

Jobscan said I should have 750 words in my resume. I don't agree with that. Even if you have fewer than 750 words in your resume, Jobscan still provides their evaluation

I clicked "Next" again, and Job Scan compared the skills and keywords in my resume to the job description.

The skills and keywords in the job description as well as their frequency are compared to the resume.

After reading the Jobscan report, I added some of the "Hard Skills" and "Soft Skills" wherever it made sense. In all, I replaced about 20 words in my resume with keywords from the job description, which Jobscan identified for me.

I then rescanned my resume and got a "77% Match Rate."

The best thing about Jobscan is that it wasn't hard at all. Compared to the time it used to take to customize my resume, customizing my resume with Jobscan was quick.

Because working with Jobscan is so easy, you'll be more likely to customize your resume in the future.

Jobscan Pricing

If you use Jobscan, you receive five free scans, monthly. So if you joined Jobscan on May 1, you'll receive another five free scans on June 1.

If you need more than five, Jobscan has two plans giving you unlimited scans. The first is $49.95 monthly. The second is $89.95 for three months, and the first month is free.

Additional Customization?

If the job you're applying for requires skills you haven't emphasized in your resume, additional modifications may be needed to get the interest of HR and the hiring manager.

While Jobscan can capture the keywords, credentials, skills, and experience required to get through the HR elimination system, Angela Rose of Hcareers.com recommends going through your Summary and removing words and phrases not specific to the position.

If possible, add additional strengths to the Summary with the most relevant first.[88]

Angela also recommends reviewing past positions and extracting from those positions skills and achievements pertaining to this position.

Update the accomplishments under the past positions to make them more relevant to the new position. Of course, remove accomplishments that are not relevant.[89]

More Ways to Customize

If you're looking for additional ways to customize your resume, you might want to consider customizing by industry, by company, and then finally — if you have this information — by hiring manager.

Industry. The best way to customize by industry is to go to websites focused on the industry and identify the most commonly used words. This can be done by copying the words from the sites and throwing them into Wordle (http://www.wordle.net/). The largest words in the Wordle output are the most commonly used words.

Next find places in your resume to add these words. You could also take the words you threw into Wordle and throw them into the job description screen in Jobscan and your resume in the resume screen. Jobscan could then tell you if you have these words in your resume already.

Company. If you'd like to customize by company, follow the same steps above but copy the words from the company website. If you are experienced in areas important to the company you are applying to, emphasize these areas in the Summary or body of the resume.

Hiring Manager. If you know who the hiring manager is, see if she has published articles online. Follow the same steps I mentioned above but use the published articles to identify the keywords that are important to her. If you find the hiring manager is very interested in a particular field where you have experience, find a way to emphasize the field in your summary and where possible, elsewhere in the resume.

Remember …

Customization isn't one of those things that's just nice to do. Tools like Jobscan were created, because companies are looking for certain keywords to determine whether you're the right match.

---

[88] Rose, Angela. "Easy Steps to Customize Your Resume for the Job You're Applying for Right Now." Hcareers.com. http://www.hcareers.com/us/resourcecenter/tabid/306/articleid/1027/default.aspx (accessed October 11, 2017).
[89] Rose.

Since you've already put in a great deal of effort to produce the strongest resume possible, and you've gone through the time-consuming effort of applying online, *you owe it to yourself to add those keywords and spell out those acronyms that will make the Applicant Tracking System select you.*

Final Checks

In the next chapter, we'll review the final steps to take before you release your resume to a hiring manager.

Before Your Resume Goes Anywhere ...

Before the resume goes anywhere, you want to ensure that it makes the best impression possible

You don't want to lose your chance because of a simple spelling error or inconsistent formatting.

As you strive to make your resume ATS-friendly and customize it for each position, you want to ensure that your resume puts you in the best possible light.

By now, you'll have created your resume, made it easy to read, and done everything possible to get it through the ATS.

If the resume is to be submitted online or given to a potential employer, you'll have also customized your resume as I described earlier.

Before you do anything more…

1) Take 10 <u>deep</u> breaths. Count each one as you inhale and exhale. (I do this at least once each day.) According to the American Institute of Stress, "Deep breathing increases the supply of oxygen to your brain, … promotes a state of calmness, … and quiets your mind."[90]

2) Use your Microsoft Word software to do a grammar and spell check. Remember, Word won't catch everything. If you misspell a word and end up spelling another word instead, spell check will not catch it.

3) After reviewing, upload your resume to a tool from The Ladders folks: http://www.theladders.com/resume. The online tool reviews your resume for effectiveness, and then it offers notations with edit suggestions, which include catching minor errors.

   a. I put a misspelled word in my resume to see if The Ladders tool could also take the place of the Word's spell check. It didn't, but it provided a lot of helpful suggestions. For example:

   b. While it gave me a green light for my Contact info, Title, Summary and Skills, of the 20 or so bullets in my resume, it identified eight where I could have quantified achievements. This is a good reminder if you're weak in this area.

   c. The tool said I did a great job with capitalizing bullet points and with resume length.

---

[90] Marksberry, Kellie. "Take a Deep Breath." http://www.stress.org/take-a-deep-breath/ (accessed October 11, 2017).

    d. It dinged me, though, because I didn't have 4 to 8 bullets for each position. While this can be helpful for some people, when you've had as many positions as I've had, it isn't always possible.

    e. It wisely pointed out 4 places where I should have added a period.

    f. Finally, it said that I wrongly used, "I" in my "Summary," which I do not agree with. It also dinged me because one of my awards had the unique name, "I Will."

4) Read your resume slowly enough so that you can focus on what you're saying. This will help you catch any errors in word choice or tense.

5) Finally, scan the resume to make sure you've used consistent formatting throughout and that everything looks as it should.

If you're thinking, "You've got to be kidding! Why do I need to go to so much trouble to create a resume?" remember the words of Martin Yate, author of *Knock 'em Dead Resumes*:

Your resume is the most financially important document you will ever own: when your resume works, you work; when it doesn't you don't.

I will add one more thought to that sentiment.

When you receive your offer, do you want just any salary or the highest salary possible?

That is why all of this effort is worth it.

To Your Success...

Achievement Stories

Getting the hiring manager's attention requires that you distinguish yourself.

Achievement Stories are an excellent way to do that because...

They are the stories behind the Work Experience in your resume...

They are a key component of a strong LinkedIn profile. (More on that in my next books.)

They are also the stories wise job seekers share in interviews to set you apart from all other candidates...(More on that in my next books.)

Now, you know how to create your Achievement Stories.

Getting to the Hiring Manager

Getting to those interviews means customizing your resume for each and every position to increase your odds of selection by the Applicant Tracking System.

Now, you know the quickest and most effective way to customize your resume.

Even if the Applicant Tracking System gives a thumbs down, now, you know there is more than one way to get in front of a hiring manager.

The Hiring Manager's Secrets

When you think about your upcoming interviews, you're no longer afraid. Now, you know what a failed interview looks like.

You also know the hiring manager's secrets, so you know what she's looking for. You can taste success.

Wisdom Leads to Success

Because you now know that not everyone you meet in your job search is looking out for you or is even well informed, you're a lot wiser.

You know who to believe and what to ignore. As a result, you'll be a more successful job seeker.

Be on the lookout for my upcoming books on LinkedIn and Interviewing Success.

Successful Job Hunting,

Clark

A Question For You...

Will this book help other job seekers?

If so, please let them know by following these steps to add your review.

1. Enter www.amazon.com in the url field.

2. Enter the book title in Amazon's search field.

3. Scroll down (about half-way) until you see Customer reviews.

4. Click on the "Write a customer review" button.

If you have suggestions please tell me.

clark.finnical@job-seekers-advocate.com

Be on the lookout for my books on

LinkedIn

and

Interviewing Success.

Thank you!

Additional Reading...

Reinventing Yourself by Steve Chandler

For many of us, recovering from job loss and getting a new job requires reinventing ourselves. No one is a better teacher than Steve Chandler.

100 Ways to Motivate Yourself by Steve Chandler

Motivation is a critical part of job seeking success.

StrengthsFinder 2.0 by Tom Rath

Taking the assessment, which is only possible after buying the book, enables you to 1.) Better understand your strengths; 2.) Include excerpts from the assessment as well as the full report in your LinkedIn Profile Summary. By doing this, others can learn about your strengths as well. See how I've used this information in the Summary of my LinkedIn Profile - https://www.linkedin.com/in/clarkfinnical/

Talking from 9 to 5: Women and Men at Work by Deborah Tannen

Understanding each other is critical while seeking work and while doing work. Deborah Tannen is the author of *You Just Don't Understand*, a New York Times bestseller for almost four years

The Practicing Mind: Bringing Discipline and Focus Into Your Life by Thomas M. Sterner

Per a Goodreads review written by Alexander Fitzgerald, the author *"makes a wonderful case for how we are all practicing at all times, and how our conduct during every activity effects us through life...A great read for anyone who needs to be more patient in their day-to-day life, or who needs to perform at a top level in their job."*

Be Smart: Sail Past the Hazards of Conventional Career Advice by Paula Asinof and Mina Brown

One of Paula's clients stated, "Paula Asinof is the best known and wisest executive communication guru in the Dallas area."

The Unwritten Rules of the Highly Effective Job Search by Orville Pierson

Orville developed the curriculum used by Lee Hecht Harrison, the largest outplacement firm in the world.

Guerrilla Marketing for Job Hunters 3.0 by David Perry and Jay C. Levinson

David Perry and Mark Haluska, one of the book's contributors, are veteran recruiters with a great deal of helpful knowledge for job seekers.

Career Coaches...

Two lines hardly do justice to the talent below. I encourage you to go to their websites to find out more.

Patricia Edwards – Career Wisdom Coach –

Patricia's experience as a Talent Manager where she selected thousands of job candidates at top companies puts her in an ideal position to advise and coach job seekers.

https://careerwisdomcoach.com/author/careerwisdomcoach/

Matt Krumrie – Resumes, Career Advice and Job Search Tips -

Matt has authored 2000+ career and job search articles for the Minneapolis Start Tribune, Ziprecruiter.com, CollegeRecruiter.com and Flexjobs.com.

http://www.resumesbymatt.com/

Paula Asinof – Yellow Brick Path -

Paula's background includes 10 years of Executive Search recruiting and Director of Career Services for Sanford-Brown College among other things.

http://www.yellowbrickpath.com/

Liz Ryan – The Human Workplace –

Liz's articles are published in Forbes. She frequently appears on national news networks. Liz Ryan was a corporate HR VP forever. She has a great website.

http://www.humanworkplace.com/

Lisa Rangel – Chameleon Resumes -

Lisa has an amazing amount of valuable information on her website. She has also been the Expert Moderator for LinkedIn's Premium Career Group since 2012

http://chameleonresumes.com/

Susan P. Joyce – For Smarter Job Search -

Susan has shown us how to identify the correct title for a role when many titles are being used. She also has a wealth of free information on her website.

https://www.job-hunt.org/

Hannah Morgan – Career Sherpa –

Hannah's experience in HR, Outplacement, Workforce Development and Career Services gives her an excellent 360 degree view of job search.

http://careersherpa.net/

Keeping The Faith…

Scriptures I Prayed While Unemployed

Personal note - when everything is ripped away from you and all you have is your faith, you cling all the harder to that faith. Through four restructures, my faith grew more and more, as I saw God carry me through very difficult times and answer my prayers.

And we know that in all things God works for the good of those who love him, who have been called according to his purpose.

Romans 8:28 (NIV)

Trust in the Lord with all your heart and lean not on your own understanding; in all your ways submit to him, and he will make your paths straight.

Proverbs 3:5-6 (NIV)

For I am the Lord your God who takes hold of your right hand and says to you, Do not fear; I will help you.

Isaiah 41:13 (NIV)

God is our refuge and strength, an ever-present help in trouble.

Psalm 46:1 (NIV)

He gives strength to the weary and increases the power of the weak.

Isaiah 40:29

So do not fear, for I am with you; do not be dismayed, for I am your God. I will strengthen you and help you; I will uphold you with my righteous right hand.

Isaiah 41:10 (NIV)

I can do all things through him who strengthens me.

Philippians 4:13 (ESV)

For God gave us not a spirit of fearfulness; but of power and love and discipline.

2 Tim 1:7 (ASV)

Acknowledgements

Special thanks go to HB, DC and CH for their patience while I wrote the book.

In addition, I am very grateful to my editor, Chris Largent, for his excellent ideas and suggestions.